# THE JOHN HARVARD LIBRARY

Howard Mumford Jones
*Editor-in-Chief*

Portrait of Christopher Colles, by John Wesley Jarvis, c. 1809.
Courtesy of the New-York Historical Society, New York City.

# A
# SURVEY OF THE ROADS
# OF THE UNITED STATES
# OF AMERICA

1789

*By*

CHRISTOPHER COLLES

Edited by Walter W. Ristow

THE BELKNAP PRESS OF
HARVARD UNIVERSITY PRESS
*Cambridge, Massachusetts*
1961

# Preface

During this twelve months some 200,000,000 road maps will be distributed to American motorists, primarily through gas stations and automobile clubs. The maps will guide vacationing families and business travelers over the nation's ever expanding network of superhighways and along less busy shaded lanes and byways.

Most speeding motorists will take for granted the scenic and scientifically engineered roads and the attractive and accurate maps that are theirs to use and enjoy. Few will give thought to the beginnings of roads and road maps in the United States.

Today's tourist reckons a day's travel at three hundred miles or more. Compare this with the following account of an American traveler when the nation was in its infancy:

> The country through which we passed was extremely dismal, being covered with forests upon which the axe had as yet made but little impression, for excepting a few open spots here and there, such trees alone were cut down as were necessary for the formation of a road, or rather the *line* of a road, for this was still in a very rude state, the driver being obliged to wind as well as he could between the remaining stumps. The soft soil being rendered deep by the rain that had fallen, our progress was very slow, not exceeding thirteen miles in four hours.[1]

The conditions here described were typical of the roads in most parts of the country when the United States Constitution was ratified in 1789, and for a decade or more thereafter (Fig. 1). Roads of all types during this period probably totaled less than 3000 miles.

To guide native, as well as foreign, travelers over a portion of this network of rocky or deep-rutted highways, there was published in 1789 the first parts of *A Survey of the Roads of the United States of America*, by Christopher Colles. Within the next several years 83 small road maps were compiled and published in the series. Collectively they mapped the major roads between Albany, New York, and Yorktown, Virginia.

[1] Thomas Twining, *Travels in America 100 Years Ago* (New York, 1894), p. 95.

v

# PREFACE

Colles' *Survey* is recognized as the earliest American road guide, and the forerunner of modern United States road maps. It is also one of the most detailed and comprehensive historical records of the United States at the time of its constitutional establishment. Because copies of the road book are preserved in but a few American libraries, Colles' *Survey* is known only to a small group of scholars. This facsimile reproduction makes available to a wider audience a most interesting and informative historical document.

The compiler and publisher of the *Survey*, Christopher Colles, is likewise unknown to most twentieth-century Americans. He merits more of posterity. Colles was one of the most gifted inventive and mechanical geniuses of his day, and one of America's earliest engineers. Details of his many-faceted, albeit economically unsuccessful, life are presented in the accompanying biographical notes.

Because of his wide range of interests and contributions in several fields, certain aspects of Colles' life have been previously presented in technical books and in professional journals. In preparing the present work, the author is indebted to earlier researchers and writers.

Colles' restless and poverty-burdened life did not permit the accumulation or retention of personal papers, and no such records are known. Contemporary data about him, therefore, must be laboriously culled from newspapers and from letters and papers of friends and associates. In pursuing an endless succession of clues and leads, the author has had the assistance and cooperation of a number of librarians and archivists.

Among those to whom grateful acknowledgment is expressed are Dr. James J. Heslin, Arthur Carlson, and Wilmer Leech of the New-York Historical Society; Robert W. Hill, Keeper of Manuscripts, and Mrs. Maud Cole of the Rare Book Division, of the New York Public Library; Clifford Shipton, Director of the American Antiquarian Society; H. Richard Archer, Custodian, Chapin Library, Williams College; Frank N. Jones, Director, Peabody Institute, Baltimore, Maryland; and Herman R. Friis, Chief Archivist, Technical Records Division, U. S. National Archives. I should like to thank the Library of Congress and Yale University Library for the use of their copies of the *Survey* in preparing this facsimile edition. I am also indebted for assistance and encouragement to my colleagues in the Manuscript, Map, and Rare Book Divisions of the Library of Congress.

The map of the Atlantic seaboard, which serves as an index to the plates in Colles' *Survey*, is the skilled and artistic work of Joseph Dunich, cartographic specialist on the staff of the U. S. Coast and Geodetic Survey.

WALTER W. RISTOW
*Library of Congress*

Fig. 1. In the young United States of the 1790's forests were still very much in evidence. This rural scene in northern New Jersey also shows typical farmsteads, fences, and roads of the period. From *New York Magazine*, Feb. 1794. Courtesy of the Library of Congress.

# CONTENTS

## PART ONE

### Christopher Colles
### Early American Engineer and Cartographer

BY WALTER W. RISTOW

| | | |
|---|---|---|
| I | Old World Background | 3 |
| II | Pre-Revolutionary Years in America | 7 |
| III | Colles' Travels and Tribulations During the War | 16 |
| IV | Inland Waterways Projects | 21 |
| V | Colles During the Critical Years 1783–1789 | 36 |
| VI | The Survey of the Roads of the United States of America | 41 |
| VII | Source Materials Used in Compiling the Road Book | 53 |
| VIII | The Erskine-DeWitt Maps and Colles' *Survey* | 73 |
| IX | Latter Years | 82 |
| X | The *Survey of the Roads,* Contemporary Guidebook and Historical Record | 96 |
| | Bibliography of Christopher Colles | 107 |
| | General Bibliography | 109 |
| | Inventory of Extant Copies of Colles' *Survey* | 115 |

## PART TWO

### A Survey of the Roads
### of the United States of America

BY CHRISTOPHER COLLES

| | |
|---|---|
| Facsimile of Original Edition (1789) | 119 |
| Alphabetical Index | 207 |
| Classified Index | 219 |
| Index to Part One | 225 |
| Index Map | folded at end |

# ILLUSTRATIONS

*Frontispiece*  Portrait of Christopher Colles, by John Wesley Jarvis

1  Rural Scene in Northern New Jersey  vii

2  Plan of Limerick, by Christopher Colles  5

3  Announcement of Geography Lectures  8

4  Advertisement for Series of Lectures on Natural Philosophy  9

5  Proposals For a Public Water System  14

6  Colles' Letter to George Washington  22

7  View on the Mohawk River  26

8  Proposals for the Speedy Settlement of the Waste and Unappropriated Lands  28

9  Invitation to a Meeting to Discuss Inland Navigation  30

10  Title Page of Timber Canal Booklet  33

11  Map Showing Proposed Route of the Timber Canal  34

12  Announcement of an Exhibit of the Solar Microscope  38

13  Diagram Illustrating the Operation of the Solar Microscope  39

14  Eighteenth-Century Perambulator  43

15  Broadside Announcing the *Survey of the Roads*  44

16  Map of New York City, 1789, Engraved by Cornelius Tiebout  47

17  Tiebout's Engraving of the Falls on the Schuylkill River  48

18  Erskine-DeWitt Map Showing the Road South from Alexandria, Va.  55

19  Road Extending Northeast of Princeton, N.J. on Erskine-DeWitt Map  56

20  Erskine-DeWitt Map 74-D, Showing a Part of New Jersey  71

ILLUSTRATIONS

21 Plate From an Eighteenth-Century Irish Road Book 74

22 Title Page of Colles' *Geographical Ledger* 78

23 A Map From the *Geographical Ledger* 80

24 Broadside Announcing a Lecture on the Semaphoric Telegraph 85

25 Title Page of Booklet Describing the Numerical Telegraph 86

26 Illustration of Colles' Numerical Telegraph 87

27 View of St. Paul's Church 91

28 Portrait of Colles, by James Frothingham 93

29 Street Scene in Philadelphia 98

30 Rural Landscape and Roads in Southeastern Pennsylvania 98

31 Gray's Ferry, Near Philadelphia 99

32 Triumphal Arch at Trenton 99

33 Early American "Stage Waggon" 102

34 Farmstead and Road Scene in Northern New Jersey 105

35 Road, Bridge, and Grist Mill Near Bergen, New Jersey 105

PART ONE

# CHRISTOPHER COLLES
# EARLY AMERICAN ENGINEER
# AND CARTOGRAPHER
*By*
*Walter W. Ristow*

# I

# Old World Background

ONE who knew him well described Christopher Colles as a "kind of living antithesis." He had, it was said, "the most diminutive frame and the most gigantic conceptions, the humblest demeanor and the boldest projects." [1] Colles' active mind teemed with bold and exciting ideas when the infant United States was ripe for innovation and development. Lack of capital, the inability to inspire those who might have given aid, and the unfavorable economic climate of the times, however, doomed his every effort.

To certain of his contemporaries Christopher Colles was a genius. Others considered him an impractical visionary. His ideas were certainly far in advance of the times. History credits him with having been the first to conceive or propose a succession of farsighted and noteworthy projects. None of his proposals, however, brought to Colles personal gain or public acclaim. It remained for others, under more favorable and enlightened circumstances, to carry through to successful accomplishment the ideas and projects that were spawned in his fertile brain.

Christopher Colles was one of those hapless individuals upon whom fate plays unkind tricks. Blessed with exceptional gifts and skills, they are inevitably prevented by some quirk of fortune from ever reaching their goals. Philosophical though he was, Colles complained on occasions that had he been trained as a hatter, men probably would have come into the world minus heads.

During his active years, Colles associated with some of the foremost men of his day. "No man," wrote Mines, "possessed more friends

[1] Gulian C. Verplanck, "Reminiscences of New York," in *The Talisman for 1830* (New York, 1829), p. 348.

3

when living." [2] But he died in poverty and loneliness, and his remains rest, unmarked, in an old New York churchyard.

Christopher Colles, though of English ancestry, was born in Dublin, Ireland, on May 9, 1739. He attended school near Kilkenny, studying under Dr. Richard Pococke, a distinguished cleric and oriental scholar. From Pococke young Colles acquired a good general education, as well as specialized training in mathematics, geography, engineering, and "natural philosophy," or science. As he advanced in his studies, Christopher became an assistant to his old master. Ever a restless soul, Colles found in Pococke a stabilizing influence.

In his early professional years Christopher's career also was guided and directed by his uncle, William Colles. After completing his studies, the young engineer worked for several years with William on the construction of a canal between Kilkenny and Inistioge. Upon the uncle's recommendation, young Colles was, in 1761, appointed pay clerk to the River Nore Navigation Board. These early experiences on waterways stirred his interest and provided experience that was utilized on the several internal improvement projects he later espoused in America.

Following his marriage to Miss Anne Keough on January 14, 1764, Colles worked for a brief period with his old tutor Dr. Pococke, who was now Bishop of Ossory. The death of the bishop in 1765 brought several unsettled years during which Colles changed jobs and residence with great frequency. Local records show that during this period children were born to him and Anne in Kilkenny, Limerick, Gillogue, and County Clare.

With the passing of Pococke, sole responsibility for guiding the career of his brilliant, but restless, nephew fell upon William Colles. This was not always an easy or rewarding task. In August 1766, for example, William wrote his daughter in London that

I have got Kit Colles (whose affairs here were in a desperate way) into an employment under one Mr. Dukart, an engineer, in which if he behaves with care I doubt not but he will do very well. Mr. Dukart likes him very much and has left him for the present to conduct the building of the Customs House in Limerick.[3]

[2] John F. Mines, *Walks in Our Churchyards* (New York, 1895), p. 139.
[3] Christopher J. Colles, "Ancestry of Christopher Colles in Ireland," in American Irish Historical Society, *Journal*, vol. 29 (1931), pp. 69–70.

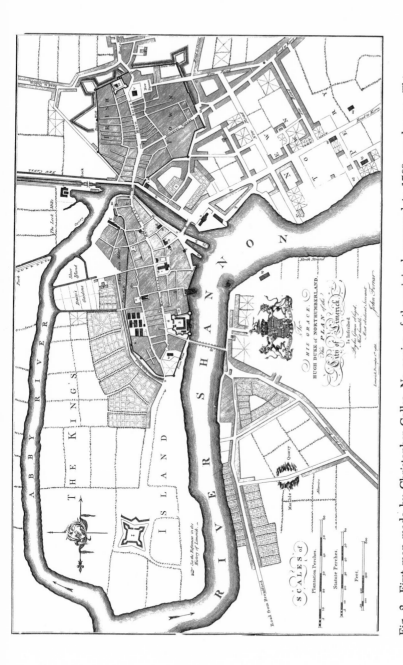

Fig. 2. First map made by Christopher Colles. No copies of the original, prepared in 1769, are known. This reproduction is from John Ferrar's *History of Limerick*, 1787. A note in the text reads "Plan of Limerick, done from an actual Survey in 1769, by Mr. Christopher Colles, for his Grace the Duke of Northumberland and reduced to a small Scale for the History of Limerick by C. J. Sauthier." Courtesy of the Library of Congress.

Christopher apparently did not behave with care, for in less than a year he was operating a stone quarry. This venture also proved to be of short duration, and in 1769 Colles was signing himself "Director of Inland Navigation of the Shannon." While in this post he found time to prepare a set of "Proposals for publishing by subscription an accurate plan of the City and Suburbs of Limerick, describing not only the present state with its new streets, etc., but also the walls, and Fortifications in their perfect condition, taken from an actual survey thereof." [4] We do not know whether or not this first venture of Colles into the field of cartography was successful. There are no extant copies of the map, but a reduced reproduction was published in 1787 in Ferrar's *History of Limerick* (Fig. 2).

The death of William Colles in March 1770 severed Christopher's last strong tie to Ireland. He decided, therefore, to emigrate to America and put to productive and profitable use his engineering training and experience. Passage money was secured from relatives, and in May 1771 Colles sailed from Cork with his wife and four children. They landed in Philadelphia on August 10, 1771, to begin life in the New World.

[4] *Ibid.*, p. 71.

# II

# Pre-Revolutionary Years in America

With four young children and a wife to support, Colles could not delay seeking employment. Three weeks after landing in Philadelphia he offered his services to the public through an advertisement in the August 26, 1771, issue of the *Pennsylvania Chronicle*. The notice read:

Mills of various kinds, and other Hydraulic Engines, designed and constructed according to the true Principles of Mechanics and Hydrostatics, Land surveyed and Levels taken for the Conveyance of Water — Buildings of several Kinds ornamented in the Grecian and Roman Manner, designed and superintended on reasonable Terms, by Christopher Colles, Engineer and Architect.

Colles further offered "to instruct young Gentlemen, at their Houses, in the different Branches of the Mathematics and Natural Philosophy."

The *Chronicle* notice apparently did not bring adequate results, for within a few months Colles was advertising public lectures. Perhaps the earliest was an announcement of a series on geography, in the January 13, 1772, *Pennsylvania Packet* (Fig. 3). In the same journal, on January 27, the young scientist returned

. . . his most sincere thanks to the company who favoured him with their countenance on Monday last at his Geographical Lecture; but as the inclemency of the weather, and other inconveniences, prevented several of his friends from attending, he proposes to repeat the same this day, precisely at eleven o'clock in the forenoon and six o'clock in the evening. . . .

The lectures apparently yielded some income, for similar notices were carried in subsequent issues of the *Packet* during the next several months. A notice on February 17, 1772, emphasized that, in the Geographical Lecture, presented in the rooms of the American Philosophical Society, "will be most clearly explained the figure, magnitude, and motion of the earth and moon, the different lengths of days and nights, the vicissitudes of the seasons, the phases of the moon, the theory of

7

# A GEOGRAPHICAL LECTURE,

## FOR THE AMUSEMENT OF THE PUBLIC.

THE SUBSCRIBER propofes to deliver a COURSE OF LECTURES upon the PLEASANT and USEFUL SCIENCE of

# GEOGRAPHY,

and to illuftrate the doctrine advanced, upon a Globe mounted on an entire new conftruction, far preferable to the ufual manner, and which he has reafon to believe, has not been exhibited in this city before. In this Lecture, will be introduced a brief, yet full elucidation of fuch part of the Planetary Syftem, as is moft intimately connected with our earth, and which is abfolutely neceffary for the more eafy comprehenfion of the fubject.

Amongft various other particulars, the Problems and Theorems in the common treatifes will be folved; the feeming abfurdity of the Antipodes, and of the motion of the earth will be inveftigated ; the caufe of day and night, and the viciffitudes of the feafons reprefented by a piece of new invented mechanifm, and the theory of the tides fully explained.

The Propofer will endeavour to difcufs the fubject in fuch a manner as may be perfectly intelligible to the meaneft capacity, and yet he hopes, fo as to afford fome fatisfaction to thofe of politenefs and erudition.

The Lecture to begin on Monday the 20th inftant, at 11 o'clock in the forenoon, and will be repeated again at 7 o'clock in the evening, at his houfe in Grey's Alley, near Dr. Thomas Bond's in Second-ftreet.

\*+\* Tickets for the Courfe, at 5 s. each, to be had of the Printer, and Propofer

## CHRISTOPHER COLLES.

Fig. 3. This notice in the January 13, 1772, issue of *The Pennsylvania Packet* announced a course of lectures on geography by Colles. Courtesy of the Library of Congress.

✤✤✤✤✤✤✤✤✤✤✤✤✤✤✤✤✤✤✤✤✤✤

# NATURAL PHILOSOPHY.

THIS day, the 23d Inſt. preciſely at 11 o'clock in the forenoon, and again at ſix o'clock in the evening, the Subſcriber, intends to deliver his SECOND LECTURE on Pneumaticks, or the ſcience of the Air, at the Philoſophical Society's Hall in Second-ſtreet, In this Courſe will be exhibited a variety of curious and entertaining experiments, on an Air-Pump, of an entire new conſtruction, lately invented by him.

From the ſimpiicity and ſmall expence of this Air-pump, and its being ſo contrived as to act as a condenſer by turning a cock, he has reaſon to believe it will meet with general approbation ; and therefore informs his friends and the public, that he can ſupply them with ſuch upon very reaſonable terms.

C. COLLES.

†‡† Tickets for the Courſe, at 5 s. each, to be had of the Printer hereof, of Meſſrs. Hall and Sellers, Printers, and of ſaid Colles in Grey's-alley, near Dr. Thomas Bond's in Second-Street.

N. B. The ſaid COLLES, if thereto encouraged, propoſes to deliver a Courſe, conſiſting of at leaſt three Lectures, upon the Practice, as well as Theory of Hydroſtatics and Hydraulics. In theſe Lectures, will be explained the gravity, preſſure and motion of fluids, with their action upon different machines, as wind and water mills, various kinds of pumps, the centrifugal and ſteam engines, and other machines for raiſing water for different purpoſes, by different powers, to the greateſt advantage : And, as ſaid COLLES has been engaged, as principal director, in ſome INLAND NAVIGATIONS and other works of that nature, and made theſe branches his particular ſtudy. He alſo intends to explain the principal parts of Hydraulic Architecture, as canals, locks, aqueducts, &c. The whole to be elucidated by working models of ſeveral engines, and more immediately adapted to point out the defects and improvements of theſe works, and for the conſideration of the artificers concerned therein.——Beſide the apparatus commonly exhibited at Hydroſtatical Lectures, the following will be ſhewn, viz.

The ſteam engine,
The centrifugal engine,
Model of a wind-mill with different kinds of ſails,
Model of an overſhot and underſhot water-mill,
Model of a piece of canal, with locks, aqueducts, and other appendages belonging to inland navigations.

As the preparation of a ſufficient apparatus to exhibit theſe lectures to advantage, will be attended with great expence, the ſaid COLLES expects, on this occaſion, a particular encouragement of his friends and the public, by taking off at leaſt 100 tickets, at One Dollar each ; and as ſoon as ſo many tickets are diſpoſed of, he will prepare the apparatus with all poſſible ſpeed.

Fig. 4. During his first year in Philadelphia Colles also presented a series of lectures on Natural Philosophy. From *The Pennsylvania Packet*, March 23, 1772. Courtesy of the Library of Congress.

the winds and tides, and the causes thereof." About a month later, a newspaper carried Colles' advertisement for a series of lectures on "Natural Philosophy" (Fig. 4).

With his active mind, keen powers of observation, and technical competence Colles, during his first two years in Philadelphia, made an excellent analysis of the needs of the youthful and underdeveloped America. He wrote in the September 22, 1773 issue of the *Pennsylvania Packet*:

In all newly established colonies it appears highly necessary to use every means to moderate the price of labour, and for carrying on all kinds of manufactures with the greatest facility, to which purpose mechanical contrivances seem particularly adapted; and as Christopher Colles, of Philadelphia, has made that branch his favorite study, he gives public notice that he has lately thought of some things, which he apprehends may be exceedingly advantageous to this country, particularly a method whereby a furnace for extracting iron ore, may be carried on in any situation remote from water . . . upon an equal footing with those, whose proximity to water make their situation convenient; and also a cheap and simple machine to raise water to Gentlemen's seats, and to water meadows, which contrivance he will execute for such as are willing to encourage him.

A similar notice was published in the September 29, 1773, issue of the *Pennsylvania Gazette*. These announcements, which suggest the competence and versatility of Colles, also indicate that he was one of America's earliest proponents of automation.

Colles' several attempts to publicize his skills resulted in some job opportunities. Thus, in the summer of 1773, he was engaged to construct a steam engine to supply water for the cooling coils of a distillery. In due course the engine was completed and operating, but it had certain mechanical deficiencies.

For the dual purpose of securing competent technical criticism and advice, as well as to obtain recognition of his invention by a learned body, Colles turned to the American Philosophical Society. In a letter addressed to the Society on August 20, 1773, he wrote:

As your society seems particularly calculated to forward all useful undertakings, I beg leave to address myself to you on the following subject: I have a long time been of opinion that *fire* might be advantageously employed as a power, to work a variety of mechanical engines, and machines, and previous to my trying any thing new in that way, I have erected one

10

very little differing from the common construction, for raising water for a distillery, & having tried a variety of experiments in order to bring the expence into a narrow compass, do find that the form & dimensions of the *boiler* are not sufficient to furnish a proper quantity of *steam* to make it operate with the necessary velocity, & as the expence has exceeded my expectation and ability, I propose making application to the public by way of subscription, for to reimburse what I have already expended, & to enable me to complete my design. But as all persons are not competent judges of the nature or utility of such contrivances, I request the favour of the Society, that such gentlemen of their body as they shall think convenient, may look at the machine and report their opinion thereof, which will enable the subscription to go on with the greater facility, & much oblige

Their most h'ble serv't.<br>Christopher Colles.[1]

The appeal for aid was also reported in the August 20, 1773, Minutes of the American Philosophical Society, along with the statement that the request was "referred to Rittenhouse, Wells, Proud & Biddle." [2] The committee members made a prompt examination of the steam engine and, on August 25, reported that they had seen it "perform several strokes, tho' some of the materials not being sufficiently large and strong, owing to his attempting the execution at a very low expence, it did not continue its motion long; but that a Steam Engine may be brought to answer the purpose of raising Water much cheaper than by Men or Horses is a fact well known, & we are of opinion that the undertaker is well acquainted with the principles of this particular branch of Mechanics & very capable of carrying it into execution & therefore worthy of Public encouragement." [3]

In the opinion of one twentieth-century engineer, Colles, because of limited funds, "made his boiler too small and of insufficient steaming quality [which resulted in the failure] to keep his engine in continuous operation." [4] The young engineer undoubtedly derived some comfort from the generally favorable report of the committee of experts. It is unlikely, however, that he received any tangible "public encouragement," and the distillery steam engine probably never was put to

---

[1] Thompson Westcott, *Life of John Fitch* (Philadelphia, 1878), p. 155.
[2] *American Philosophical Society: Early Proceedings . . . From the Manuscript Minutes of its Meetings from 1744 to 1838* (Philadelphia, 1884), p. 82.
[3] *Ibid.*, Minutes of August 25, 1773, p. 83.
[4] Greville Bathe, *An Engineer's Miscellany* (Philadelphia, 1938), p. 122.

practical and continued use. Nonetheless, for this effort Colles is credited by some authorities, among them Thompson Westcott, the biographer of John Fitch, as being "the first man, it is believed, who *constructed* a steam-engine in America." [5]

In intervals between engineering assignments, Colles continued to derive income from public lectures. Sometime in 1773 there was printed, by John Dunlap of Philadelphia, a "Syllabus of a Course of lectures in Natural Experimental Philosophy, by Christopher Colles." Eighteen lectures were listed, on such varied topics as mechanics, pneumatics, hydrostatics, hydraulics, geography, and astronomy. The broadside attested that "these lectures will be delivered in an easy familiar style, entirely free from affected terms, explained and illustrated by experiments upon a variety of Apparatus and Machinery."

By the early seventies the American Philosophical Society had become an active and influential organization, with a distinguished and learned membership. With his wide interests and intellectual curiosity Colles undoubtedly was attracted to the Society and its members. We have noted already that some of his public lectures were presented in the Society's rooms, and that he had called upon a committee of its members to advise him on the steam engine. We can be sure that he attended public meetings and lectures of the Society. The officers of the American Philosophical Society, for reasons unknown, did not, however, invite his membership.

This was undoubtedly a deep disappointment to Colles and, coupled with the failure of the steam engine, may have contributed to his decision to leave Philadelphia. The innate restlessness of the gifted engineer, and the hope of finding greater opportunities for his talents in the growing city at the mouth of the Hudson very likely also induced the change of residence. Whatever the reason, toward the end of 1773, or early 1774, the Colles family moved to New York City.

First record of their presence there is an announcement of a series of public lectures by Colles, which was published in the March 10, 1774, issue of *Rivington's New York Gazetteer*. The talks, on "natural and experimental philosophy," were probably the same ones previously given in Philadelphia.

Christopher Colles was not the first person to present lectures on

[5] Westcott, *John Fitch*, p. 153.

technical and scientific subjects in America. His contributions in this field did, however, help promote and advance the cause of public education. Moreover, the lectures provided a regular, though small, supplementary income. The public meetings also made Colles one of the best-known personalities in New York City. "They were," wrote Mines, "an unfailing matter of interest and entertainment to the New Yorkers of the [late eighteenth] century and though they did not benefit himself to any great extent, they paved the way for others who reduced theory to practice and thus permanently benefited the community." [6]

The lack of a public water supply was one of the things which early impressed Colles about New York City. Characteristically, he determined to do something about it. Shortly after his arrival he proposed to the city administrators that a steam pumping station and reservoir be erected. The plan for the water system was outlined in a broadside addressed "To the Worshipful The Mayor, Aldermen, and Commonalty, Of the City of New-York, in Common Council convened" (Fig. 5).

The suggestion was favorably received and the *New York Gazette and Weekly Mercury*, for August 1, 1774, reported that "Last Thursday sen'night the Corporation of the City met, and agreed to Mr. Christopher Colles's Proposal for supplying this City with fresh Water, by Means of a Steam Engine, Reservoir, and Conduit Pipes. . . . The water will be conveyed through every Street and Lane . . . with a perpendicular Conduit Pipe at every Hundred yards, at which Water may be drawn at any Time of the Day or Night."

Colles' plan involved digging a series of deep wells, from which water would be pumped by steam engine to a reservoir near the Collect Pond. The pipes, it should be noted, were bored pine logs. The water system, with a capacity of 200 gallons per minute, was well on the way to completion in 1776, when the outbreak of the Revolutionary War forced its abandonment.

Probably because of his ever-present economic need, as well as his superabundance of ideas and energy, Colles seldom limited himself to one activity or enterprise. While seemingly weighed down with the task of getting the water supply project under way, he was also

[6] Mines, *Walks*, p. 138.

13

As the feveral Inhabitants of this City are particularly interefted in the following Affair, it is therefore judged proper to lay the fame before them.

COPY OF A

# P R O P O S A L

Of CHRISTOPHER COLLES,

For furnifhing the City of *New-York* with a conftant Supply of Fresh Water.

To the Worshipful

## The MAYOR, ALDERMEN, and COMMONALTY,

Of the City of New-York, in Common Council convened.

THE numerous and important Advantages which great and populous Cities derive from a plentiful Supply of frefh Water, requires a general Attention; and as this City is very deficient in this Article,

# CHRISTOPHER COLLES,

HUMBLY offers his Services to erect a Refervoir on the open Ground near the New Gaol, of One Hundred and Twenty-fix Feet Square, with a good Bank of Earth furrounded with a good Brick or Stone Wall Twelve Feet high, and capable of holding One Million Two Hundred Thoufand Gallons of Water; which will be of exceeding Utility in Cafe of Fire, which all Cities are liable to. To erect a Fire-Engine in a good Brick or Stone Houfe cover'd with Tiles, capable of raifing into the faid Refervoir Two Hundred Thoufand Gallons of Water in Twenty-four Hours. To lay Four Feet deep through the Broad-Way, Broad-Street, Naffau-Street, William-Street, Smith-Street, Queen-Street, and Hanover-Square, a main Pipe of good Pitch Pine of fix Inches Bore, well hooped at one End with Iron; and through every other Street, Lane and Alley in the City South Weft of Murray's-Street, King George's-ftreet, Banker's-Street, and Rutger's-Street, the like Kind of Pipe of Three Inches Bore, with a perpendicular Pipe and a Cock at every Hundred Yards of faid Pipes,---a proper Contrivance to prevent the fame from Damage by Froft; and alfo on every Wharf a convenient Pipe and Cock to fupply the Shipping. The Whole to be completely finifhed in a workmanlike Manner within two Years from the Time of making the Agreement, for the Sum of Eighteen Thoufand Pounds New-York Currency, by

### CHRISTOPHER COLLES.

The following Calculation fhewing the Utility of the above Defign, will, it is imagined, be found upon Infpection as fair and accurate as the Nature of fuch Things will admit.

It is fuppofed there are 3000 Houfes that receive Water from the Tea Water Men; that at the leaft, upon an Average, each Houfe pays One Penny Half-penny per Day for this Water; this makes the Sum of £. 6750 per Annum, which is 45s. for each Houfe per Ann. According to the Defign propofed, there will be paid £. 6000 per Ann. for four Years, which is 40s. each Houfe: By which it appears, that even whilft the Works are paying for, there will be a faving made to the City of £. 750 per Ann. and after the faid 4 Years, as the Tax will not be more than 10s. per Annum to be paid by each Houfe, it is evident that there will be faved to the City the yearly Sum of £. 5250, for ever.

In this Calculation it is fuppofed that 40s. per Ann. is to be paid for 4 Years, but this is done only to provide againft any unforefeen difficulties that may occur. It is imagined that that Sum paid 3 Years will effect the Bufinefs. The great Plenty of the Water, and its fuperior Quality, are Advantages which have not been before fpecified, but muft appear of confiderable Moment to every judicious Perfon.

*NEW-YORK*: Printed by HUGH GAINE, in HANOVER-SQUARE.

---

Fig. 5. This broadside, outlining proposals for a public water supply system, was published in June or July of 1774, shortly after Colles' arrival in New York City. Courtesy of Chapin Library, Williams College.

seeking to initiate new ventures. Thus, the Minutes of New York's Committee of Safety reported, on October 19, 1776, "a petition of Christian [sic] Colles for forty or fifty Pounds to enable him to set up his wire-works." [7]

Two weeks later, on November 4, 1776, the Minutes recorded a motion "that the sum of thirty Pounds be advanced to Mr. Christopher Collis [sic], for the purpose of enabling him to make wire and wool cards; that he, at any time, shall satisfy the Convention or Committee of Safety with regard to the progress he shall make in the business, and execute his bond to the President of this Committee for the payment thereof at the end of nine months from this day." [8] The question was put to a vote, but for reasons unstated the Committee acted unfavorably on the recommendation.

It was probably shortly thereafter that Colles, with other American patriots, abandoned New York City and fled before the approaching British Army.

[7] *American Archives*, 5th ser., vol. 3 (Washington, D. C., 1853), p. 259.
[8] *Ibid.*, p. 284.

# III

# Colles' Travels and Tribulations During the War

Wars have a disruptive effect upon the lives of people, be they men of importance or persons of lesser rank. The Revolution was no exception, and many Americans who chose to cast their lot with the patriots were forced to leave their homes and jobs. Among those who fled before the despised redcoats were Christopher Colles and his family. The difficult and unsettled war years brought untold hardship to the dispossessed engineer and his dependents, and on several occasions, they found it necessary to change their residence. For this reason, as well as because most of the normal publication outlets were curtailed, information about Colles during this period is extremely scarce.

A study of his immediate post-war interests and activities, supplemented by the few scraps of recorded data, enable us to reconstruct, with reasonable assurance, some of Colles' experiences during these troubled years.

John Colles, Christopher's cousin who arrived in New York in October 1778, wrote to a brother in Ireland that he had "enquired for Christopher who was coming on well, but this unfortunate dispute has made him fly up the country with the rest of the inhabitants, and the last person who saw him tells me he and his wife with his helpless charge were seen crossing into the Jerseys. This is all I can learn of him. His waterworks were almost finished when he fled." [1]

While still in New York, Colles actively embraced the cause of the patriots. Shortly after settling in the city he seems to have made the acquaintance of John Lamb, one of the most ardent of the Sons of Liberty and later a foremost artillery officer in the Continental Army.

Lamb's father, Anthony, was a skilled maker of mathematical instruments, and for a time John served as an apprentice. Quite likely Colles

[1] Emily J. DeForest, *James Colles, 1788–1883* (New York, 1926), pp. 14–15.

and John first met when the former visited the instrument shop to have a part constructed for one of his many inventions or appliances. During the years which culminated in the Revolutionary War, John Lamb wrote a number of anti-British pamphlets and corresponded with other patriots in Boston, Baltimore, and Philadelphia.

After the capture of Ticonderoga, Lamb offered his services to the Continental Congress. His early training with his father had provided him with a background of mathematics and science, and this knowledge "had been much cultivated and improved by an intimate association with Christopher Colles." [2] Although Colles was then busily occupied on the New York water works project, he found time "to impart a portion of his knowledge to his friend and pupil, and presented him with a valuable treatise on gunnery, of which he [Lamb] afterwards made good use." [3]

On the strength of his newly-acquired knowledge, Lamb received a commission as captain of artillery in the New York militia. He accompanied General Schuyler on the return to Ticonderoga in the summer of 1775, and was badly wounded and captured in the unsuccessful assault on Quebec. Released on parole in September 1776 Lamb was, in the following January, included in an exchange of prisoners. Shortly thereafter he was promoted to lieutenant-colonel and placed under the command of General Henry Knox, artillery commander of the Continental Army.

Lamb distinguished himself in numerous campaigns and battles, including the decisive victory at Yorktown. He had so well mastered the principles of gunnery, first taught him by Colles, that it is said that "the skill exhibited in the service of the American batteries astonished their more experienced allies." [4]

Some accounts of Colles' life credit him with having served, early in the war, as a lecturer on gunnery to artillery troops of the Continental Army. No evidence has been found to indicate that he ever had such an official assignment. Most probably, his contribution along these lines, was limited to the instruction he gave to Lamb and perhaps to a few other artillery officer prospects. Later in the war he may have

[2] Isaac Q. Leake, *Memoir of the Life and Times of General John Lamb* (Albany, 1857), p. 105.
[3] *Ibid.*, p. 106.
[4] *Ibid.*, p. 281.

had further opportunity, through Lamb, to lend his knowledge and assistance to the American cause.

As we have seen, Colles' work on the New York water supply project continued until the city was abandoned to the British in the fall of 1776. Because of his close association with Lamb, Colles no doubt considered it prudent to remove his family from the city.

While the flight, as indicated in the letter of John Colles, may initially have been into New Jersey, Christopher and his charges apparently did not remain long in that state. Our next positive record locates him in Kingston, New York. While in Albany in October 1777, Col. Lamb learned that his old friend Christopher Colles had fled from New York to Kingston for safety. When Kingston was wantonly burned by the British under Gen. John Vaughn in October 1777, Colles was again forced to flee. In a letter to Lamb, reporting the incident, Col. Eleazer Oswald noted that "I have sent Banks, [of the Commissary Department] up for little Colles who has lost his all, the wanton villains having destroyed his property which though small, to him is as great a loss as if he had been deprived of 1000£." [5]

We do not know why Colles sought refuge in Kingston. It may have been because the government of New York State was established there following the evacuation of New York. With a population of between three and four thousand, Kingston was in 1777 the third largest city in the state, exceeded only by New York and Albany.

It is possible, too, that Colles, with his engineering skill, hoped to find employment on one of the several projects concerned with fortifying the Hudson highlands and constructing barriers across the river to deter British war ships. If Colles was so employed it was apparently as a civilian, for no record of military service has been found for him. Leake's account of the Kingston fire, moreover, refers to Colles as a "noncombatant." Colles is known to have been physically frail and, for this reason as well as his age (38 years at the time), he was probably unfit for active military service.

Where Colles took refuge following the burning of Kingston is not known, nor are we informed as to how he spent the next several years. That they were years of extreme hardship for him and his family is

[5] *Ibid.*, p. 188, and manuscript letter dated Oct. 26, 1777, from Col. Eleazer Oswald to John Lamb, in New-York Historical Society collections.

evident in his petition to the New York City Council in October 1784. In one of several attempts to collect payment due for his work on the pre-war water works project, Colles stated that "in common with other citizens, friends of society and the interest of mankind, [he] suffered the most poignant afflictions during the late war, and with the utmost difficulty procured the common necessities for his family." [6]

Colles' preoccupation with inland waterways and cartography projects, in the years immediately following the Revolution, offers some clue to his wartime activities. Accounts of his life credit him with having been employed as a surveyor by the government. No verification of such occupation during the war has been found, however. One might assume that Colles' interest in surveying and maps brought him in contact with Robert Erskine and Simeon DeWitt, successive Surveyors-General to Washington's army. There is, however, no evidence of any association, by Colles, with either of these men.

Some accounts of his life state that during the war years Colles journeyed through the unsettled regions of Pennsylvania and upper New York. Verification of such trips comes from his long-time friend, the distinguished physician and teacher, Dr. John W. Francis. Writing in 1835, Francis recalled that "as there were many periods when [Colles] could not study . . . the propensities of his old master [i.e., Dr. Pococke] roused him to new efforts as a traveller. He wandered through divers parts of Pennsylvania and [New York] State, until he, by personal examination and calculations, prepared a Book of Roads . . . which he published in 1789." [7] Although Francis does not give the dates for such travels, in the chronology of Colles prior to 1789 there is no period other than during the war in which they might have been taken.

The record is not clear as to whether Colles' travels were planned expeditions or forced movements necessitated by seeking refuge from the shifting tides of the war. It seems unlikely that a man of forty, not particularly robust and with no financial resources, could have ventured

---

[6] New York City Common Council, Minutes of October 27, 1784, in Edward H. Hall, "The Catskill Aqueduct," chap. iv of "Early Pipe Line Projects, Christopher Colles' Water-works," in American Scenic and Historic Preservation Society, *Twenty-third Annual Report* (Albany, 1918), p. 701.

[7] John W. Francis, "Reminiscences of Christopher Colles," in *Knickerbocker Gallery* (New York, 1855), p. 199.

alone, or in a small party, through the semi-wilderness regions of interior Pennsylvania and upper New York State. Besides the physical obstacles, he would have had to face the danger of attack by hostile Indians, incited and goaded by American Tories and British military authorities.

It would be convenient to assume that Colles accompanied one of the units of General John Sullivan's army which in 1779 conducted a retaliatory campaign against the Indians and British sympathizers in Pennsylvania and New York. There is no support for such an assumption, however. If Colles profited from the geographical information resulting from the Sullivan campaign, it was probably through acquaintances who accompanied the expedition or from reading accounts about it.

We must conclude, therefore, that the travels which Colles engaged in during the Revolution were related to seeking refuge and securing the means of subsistence for himself and family. Initially, as has been seen, he fled across New Jersey and settled for a time in Kingston, New York. When that town was burned in the late fall of 1777, he may have fled up the Hudson to Albany or found temporary asylum in one of the other towns or villages in the Hudson highlands.

Not long after the burning of Kingston, Colles reestablished contact with his old friend John Lamb, who was now an artillery colonel. It is not unlikely that through Lamb and General Henry Knox, the latter's superior, Colles obtained employment with the Artillery Department of the Continental Army. Certain of his wartime travels may have been related to such work and to the shifting of the headquarters dictated by the expediencies of the war. There is reasonable certainty that Colles' wanderings extended up and down the Hudson valley, into eastern Pennsylvania, and northern New Jersey, and very possibly, to western Connecticut. In addition to any official surveying activities, the energetic and resourceful Colles undoubtedly made personal surveys of the roads in the various regions in which he was for a time located.

# IV

# Inland Waterways Projects

THE interest in waterways, which occupied much of Colles' attention in the first decade or so after the war, was undoubtedly stimulated by his work, travel, and studies during the Revolution. The war was not yet over when he made his first internal improvement proposal.

The plan, to remove navigation obstructions on the upper Ohio River, was initially outlined in a letter to George Washington, dated January 17, 1783. From Morristown, New Jersey, where he was then located, Colles wrote:

As the subject of this Letter is a matter which may turn out of considerable utility to the United States in general, & the state of Virginia in particular, I hope you will pardon the liberty I take of addressing myself to your Excellency.

I have lately seen Cap$^n$. Hutchins's map of Virginia, & observe that the River Ohio is navigable for large vessels from Fort Pitt to its confluence with the Mississippi, & from thence to the Ocean, except a small distance of 2 or 3 miles where it is obstructed with rapids; and as I have made Inland Navigations & other branches of Civil Engineering my study, & executed some works in Ireland with success, I do conceive it a matter of the utmost consequence to remove these obstructions; & am of opinion I am capable of effecting it at a small expence; And do propose taking a journey into Virginia to communicate my designs to the Legislature for their concurrence & encouragement; & tho these designs cannot be put in execution during the war, It may perhaps be judged expedient to make a law & establish a Company who may forward them as soon as peace is settled; I therefore request your Excellency will favour me with the names of such Gentlemen in Virginia as you may judge proper I should apply to on this affair.

As I have not the honour of a personal acquaintance with your Excellency I must request the favour of you to enquire my Character of General Knox Colonel Lamb & Colonel Hamilton.

I have communicated the outline of my plan to Mr. Henry Remsen of Morristown, who so far approved of it that he thought it advisable I should address myself to your Excellency & request your patronage.

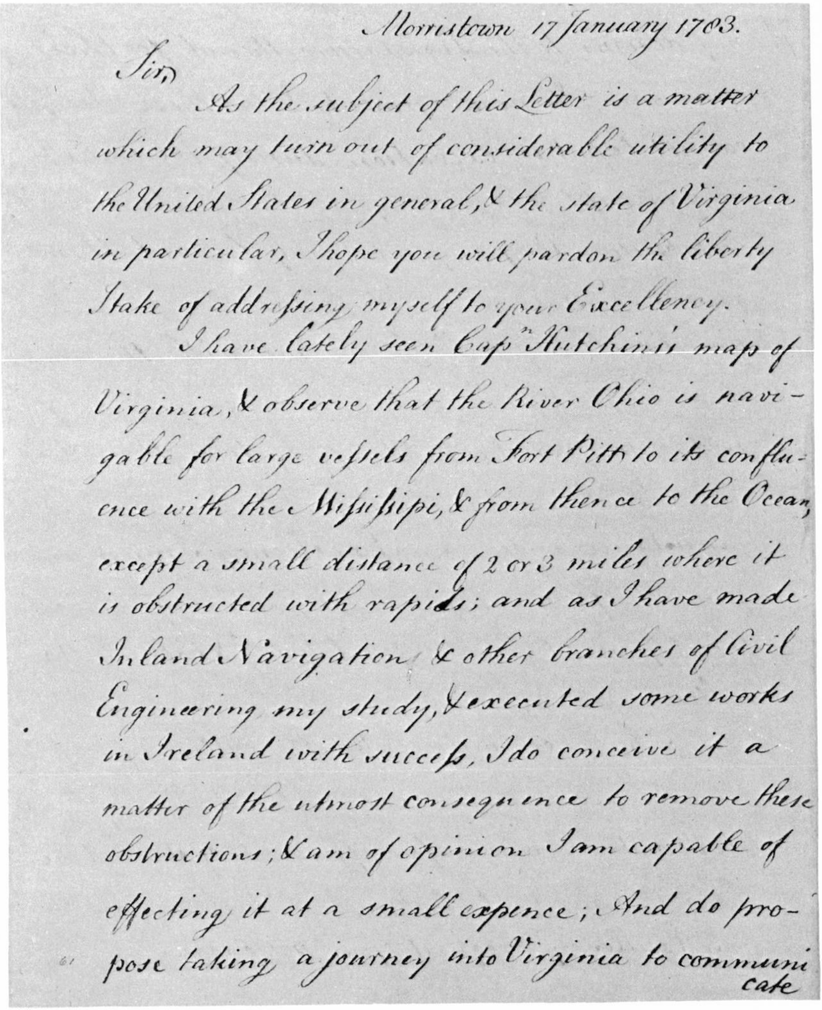

*Morristown 17 January 1783.*

Sir,

As the subject of this Letter is a matter which may turn out of considerable utility to the United States in general, & the state of Virginia in particular, I hope you will pardon the liberty I take of addressing myself to your Excellency.

I have lately seen Cap.ᵗ Hutchins's map of Virginia, & observe that the River Ohio is navigable for large vessels from Fort Pitt to its confluence with the Mississipi, & from thence to the Ocean, except a small distance of 2 or 3 miles where it is obstructed with rapids; and as I have made Inland Navigation & other branches of Civil Engineering my study, & executed some works in Ireland with success, I do conceive it a matter of the utmost consequence to remove these obstructions; & I am of opinion I am capable of effecting it at a small expence; And do propose taking a journey into Virginia to communicate

Fig. 6. Christopher Colles' letter to George Washington, dated January 17, 1783, displays a neat hand and signature, and gives some of the best clues to the activities of the hard-pressed engineer during the Revolutionary War. Courtesy of the Library of Congress.

77 my designs to the Legislature thereof for their concurrence & encouragement; & tho these designs cannot be put in execution during the war, It may perhaps be judged expedient to make a law & establish a Company who may forward them as soon as peace is settled; I therefore request your Excellency will favour me with the names of such Gentlemen in Virginia as you may judge proper I should apply to on this affair.

As I have not the Honor of a personal acquaintance with your Excellency I must request the favour of you to enquire my Character of General Knox Colonel Lamb & Colonel Hamilton.

I have communicated the outline of my plan for executing this design to Mr Henry Remsen of Morristown, who so far approved of it that he thought it advisable I should address myself to your Excellency & request your patronage.

Your Excellencys Answer directed to his care in Morristown will be gratefully received by

Your Excellencys most Obedt and most humble Servt Christopher Colles

Your Excellency's Answer directed to his care in Morristown will be gratefully received by

Your Excellency's most obdt
and most humble Servt
Christopher Colles.[1]

In this letter Colles gives some of the best clues regarding his war-time occupations and relations. It definitely establishes that he had no personal or official contact with Washington. The military personnel he lists as references (i.e., Hamilton, Knox, and Lamb) were all at one time or another attached to the Artillery Department of the Continental Army. This lends support to the theory that Colles' wartime contributions were confined to this branch. There is no intimation that Colles made maps for Washington's staff or had any association with the Geographer's Department, headed successively by Robert Erskine and Simeon DeWitt. The assumption that Colles' waterways proposals were based on personal travel during the war is disproved, particularly with respect to western Pennsylvania. The place of origin of the letter, Morristown, indicates that, in the closing months of the war at least, Colles was located in New Jersey. Lastly, the letter confirms that the intellectually curious Colles utilized some of his time during the war in research and study on the geography and resources of the country and in planning post-war projects.

In his reply, sent from Morristown on January 26, 1783, Washington informed Colles that the proposal "is, I believe, not only practical in itself, but if executed, would hereafter be of immense value in its consequences: . . . but from the present juvenile state of the Country, the abundance of land, the scarcity of labourers, and the want of resources, I say from these and many other circumstances, it appears to me that this is too early a day for accomplishing such great undertakings; and that it would be more advisable to turn your attention and abilities to works of more immediate public utility." [2]

This was obviously good counsel from one who knew, through

---

[1] George Washington, *Papers*, vol. 214, 1783, Jan. 7–Jan. 26 (MS., Library of Congress, Manuscript Division).

[2] George Washington, *Writings . . . From the Original Manuscript Sources, 1745-1799 . . .* , ed. John C. Fitzpatrick (Washington, 1931–1944), XXVI, 64–65.

personal travels, the trans-Appalachian country, and who had had experience with inland waterways projects. Colles did not, however, immediately abandon his idea, although failure to receive Washington's endorsement apparently made him decide against traveling to Virginia to present the matter to the state legislature.

Several months later the proposal was submitted to the Continental Congress. The *Journal* of that body, dated July 4, 1783, reports a favorable vote "that the petition of Christopher Colles, relative to the Navigation of the Ohio be read in Congress."[3] There is no further reference to the proposal, and we must conclude that this Colles brainchild was a stillbirth.

Colles moved back to New York City toward the end of 1783 or early 1784. First post-war record of his presence there is in the April 14, 1784, Minutes of the City Council wherein it is "agreed that Christopher Colles be permitted to occupy and use the Room in the north End of the Building commonly called the Exchange until further order of the Corporation."[4] It is probable that Colles desired the rooms to reestablish himself in some gainful enterprise or occupation. Whether it was because of his obvious need or through the intervention of influential friends that he was permitted to use space in a public building, we are uninformed.

Colles was destitute upon his return to New York. He, therefore, filed a claim for money owed him for his work on the pre-war New York water system. In October 1784, he petitioned the New York City Council for £450, the balance due him on the project. The request, as previously cited, emphasized the financial hardship Colles experienced during the Revolution. It also noted that "being now returned to the city, where he hopes to devote the remainder of his days in promoting the welfare of the city and country, he prays the corporation to use their endeavors to pay him the balance above referred to, by which he may be enabled to support his numerous family in credit, and in some degree of comfort."[5] The Council did not question the justice

[3] Continental Congress, *Journal*, vol. 24, July 4, 1783.

[4] In American Scenic and Historic Preservation Society, *Seventeenth Annual Report* (1912), p. 479.

[5] New York City Common Council, Minutes of Oct. 27, 1784, in Edward H. Hall, "Early Pipeline Projects, Christopher Colles' Water-works," American Scenic and Historic Preservation Society, *Twenty-third Annual Report* (1918), p. 702.

of Colles' claim, but there was uncertainty as to the amount due him because the early records had been destroyed.

Not receiving action on his appeal, the hard-pressed engineer renewed it on July 20, 1785, and was rewarded with a grant of £100 on account. The money obviously went fast, for on November 23 of the

Fig. 7. Christopher Colles early recognized the importance of improving navigation on the Mohawk River. From *New York Magazine*, March 1793. Courtesy of the Library of Congress.

same year he petitioned the Council for an additional £50. This request noted that Colles had "erected a horse-mill and other works for the purpose of carrying on in this City the Manufacture of Fig Blue which manufacture he proposes to have carried on by his eldest son in case he shall be engaged in the prosecution of the navigation of the Mohawk River." [6] As usual, the energetic Colles had several irons in the fire. The November 1785 petition was granted, and in January 1788 Colles accepted £50 as final settlement of all his claims.[7]

Failure to secure support for the Ohio River improvement proposal was a deep disappointment. Colles was, however, still firmly convinced of the need for improving the inland waterways of the country. Thus,

[6] New York City Common Council, Minutes of Nov. 23, 1785, *ibid.*, p. 702.
[7] *Ibid.*, p. 702.

shortly after his return to New York, he advanced another proposal (Fig. 7). This time he looked for support to the New York State Legislature.

On November 3, 1784, as recorded in the Assembly *Journal*, "a petition of Christopher Colles, was read, and referred to Mr. Adgate, Mr. Paine, Mr. Remsen, Mr. Thompson and Mr. Harper." [8]

The Committee reported back on November 6 that:

It is [its] opinion . . . that the laudable proposals of Mr. Colles, for removing the obstructions in the Mohawk river, so that boats of burthen may pass the same merit encouragement; but that it would be inexpedient for the legislature to cause that business to be undertaken at public expence.

That as the performing of such a work will be very expensive, it is therefore the opinion of the Committee, that if Mr. Colles, with a number of adventurers (as by him proposed) should undertake it, they ought to be encouraged by a law, giving and securing unto them, their heirs and assigns forever, the profits that may arise by the transportation.[9]

Again, encouraging words for the persistent engineer, but no practical aid.

Christopher Colles was not one to be deterred by a single rebuff, and he was back with his cherished project when the 1785 Legislature convened. The Committee, to which the project was referred, agreed:

That the proposed undertaking of the memorialist ought to meet with every possible encouragement; that the Committee do therefore recommend that . . . the treasurer of the State . . . advance to the memorialist the sum of Fifty Pounds, in order to enable him to make an essay; and that he lay a draft thereof before the legislature at their next meeting, that they may be enabled to determine with more precision whether the undertaking be practical or not.[10]

At last, Colles had some tangible support. With the funds thus provided he conducted a survey, most likely during the summer of 1785, along the Mohawk River as far as Wood Creek. It is possible that his jaunts during the Revolution had previously taken him into the Mohawk region. He undoubtedly, too, had studied maps of that country and read with care descriptive accounts of its geography and waterways.

[8] New York State Assembly, *Journal*, Nov. 3, 1784, p. 35.
[9] *Ibid.*, Nov. 6, 1784, p. 41.
[10] *Ibid.*, April 5, 1785, p. 135.

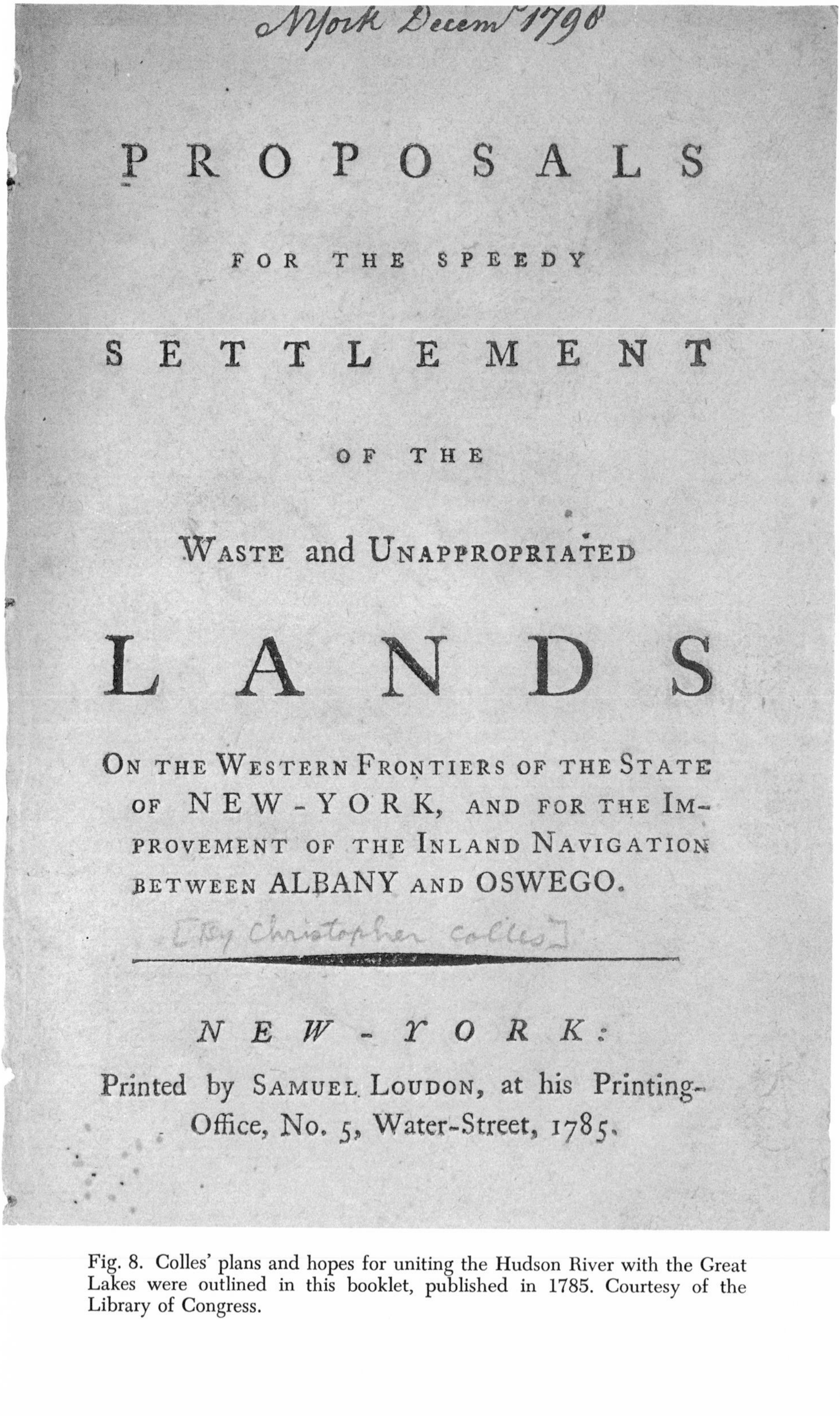

*N.York Decemr 1798*

# PROPOSALS

## FOR THE SPEEDY

## SETTLEMENT

### OF THE

## WASTE and UNAPPROPRIATED

# L A N D S

On the Western Frontiers of the State
of N E W - Y O R K, and for the Improvement of the Inland Navigation
between ALBANY and OSWEGO.

*[By Christopher Colles]*

## N E W - Y O R K:

Printed by SAMUEL LOUDON, at his Printing-
Office, No. 5, Water-Street, 1785.

Fig. 8. Colles' plans and hopes for uniting the Hudson River with the Great
Lakes were outlined in this booklet, published in 1785. Courtesy of the
Library of Congress.

All this information was presented in Colles' *Proposals For the Speedy Settlement of the Waste and Unappropriated Lands on the Western Frontiers of the State of New York, and for the Improvement of the Inland Navigation Between Albany and Oswego* (Fig. 8). Published in 1785 by Samuel Loudon of New York, the report proposed establishment of a company, with a capitalization of $13,000, empowered to prosecute the work and to be permitted to collect tolls and to receive a grant of 250,000 acres of western land. It further provided:

That Christopher Colles will transact the business of Engineer, in consideration of 5 per cent of the lands remaining in the Company's hands after the workmen's lots are laid out, and a like proportion of the lock duties.[11]

In the *Proposals* Colles displayed keen vision and an excellent knowledge of geography. He predicted that if the improvements to navigation were completed:

The internal trade will be increased — by this also the foreign trade will be promoted — by this the country will be settled — by this a variety of articles as masts, yards, and ship-timber may be brought to New York, which will not bear the expence of land carriage, and which notwithstanding will be a very considerable remittance to Europe — by this in time of war provisions and military stores may be moved with facility in sufficient quantity to answer any emergency, and by this in time of peace all the necessaries, conveniences, and if we please the luxuries of life, may be distributed to the remotest parts of the Great Lakes.[12]

While waiting for the Legislature to convene, Colles sought in December 1785 to marshal support for the Mohawk navigation project from influential citizens of New York City. For this purpose he invited a number of such persons to meet with him at the Coffee-House (Fig. 9).

The Colles report was referred to a committee of the Legislature. On March 8, 1786, the Committee informed the Assembly that it had conferred with [Colles] upon the subject of opening the navigation of the Mohawk River; and are of opinion, that the said Christopher

---

[11] Christopher Colles, *Proposals for the Speedy Settlement of the Waste and Unappropriated lands . . .* (New York, 1785), p. 6.
[12] *Ibid.*, p. 10.

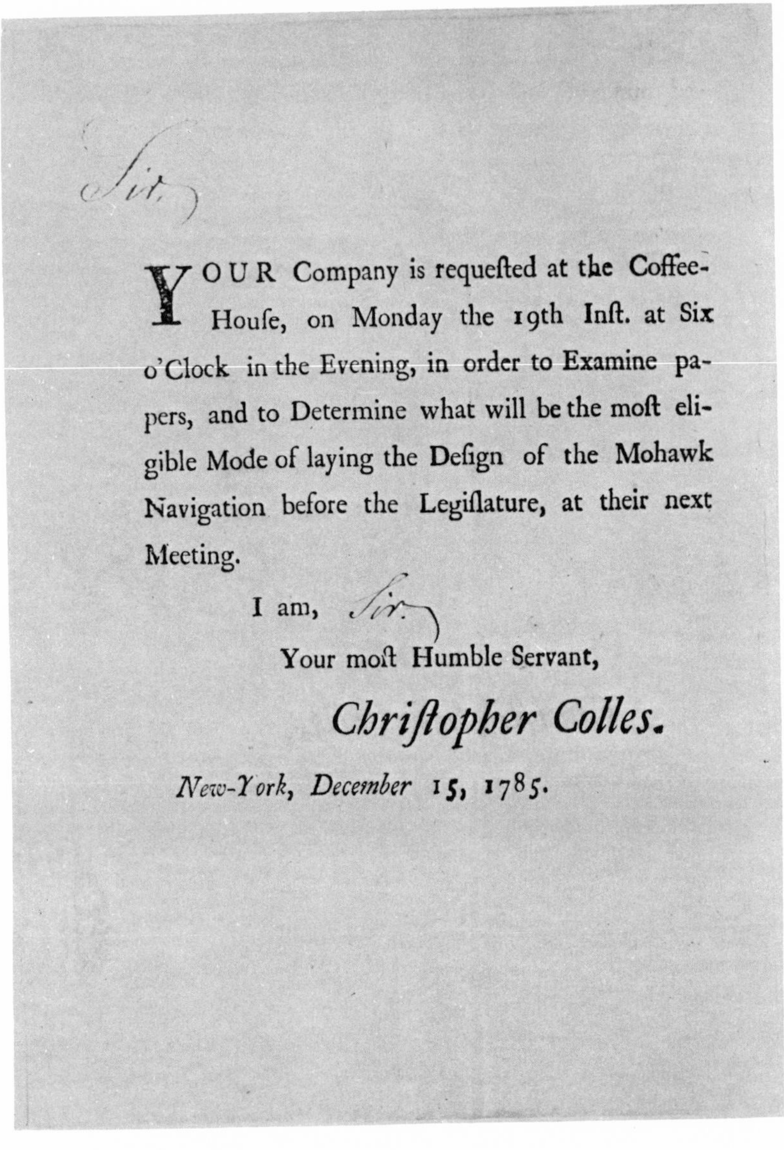

*Sir,*

**Y**OUR Company is requefted at the Coffee-Houfe, on Monday the 19th Inft. at Six o'Clock in the Evening, in order to Examine papers, and to Determine what will be the moft eligible Mode of laying the Defign of the Mohawk Navigation before the Legiflature, at their next Meeting.

I am, *Sir,*

Your moft Humble Servant,

*Chriftopher Colles.*

*New-York, December* 15, 1785.

Fig. 9. In 1785 Colles was still hopefully promoting his proposal for improving the navigation along the Mohawk Valley. Courtesy of the New-York Historical Society, New York City.

Colles and his associates, have leave to bring in a bill agreeable to the prayer of the said memorial." [13]

Once more, there were encouraging words for Colles, but they were no substitute for financial support. In 1786, New York, and the young United States, were in the trough of the post-Revolution economic depression. DeWitt Clinton, some years later, wrote that following the 1786 recommendation of the legislative committee:

> It does not appear that any further steps were taken on the part of Mr. Colles. His operations probably failed for the want of subscribers to the contemplated association.[14]

Clinton added that "it is not a little remarkable that this project commenced so soon after the termination of the revolutionary war."

In his report to the legislature, the philosophic Colles observed that "there is a critical conjuncture in most undertakings, when the smallest unforeseen discouragement sinks them at least for that age, as the lightest additional assistance would set them afloat." [15] Unfortunately for Colles and for the country, the waterway project could not withstand the rough economic storms of the time, and four more decades passed before the waters of the Great Lakes were joined with those of the Atlantic Ocean.

After 1786 Colles seems to have had no direct connection with a New York waterway project. As opportunity permitted he did, however, continue to educate and inspire others concerning its significance and importance. Among those who were moved by his earnest appeal was DeWitt Clinton who, as Governor of New York State, guided to successful realization the fond dream of Christopher Colles.

The farseeing engineer did not live to witness the opening of the Erie Canal, nor to receive the commendation of historians for having been the first to present to the public a practical and feasible plan for an inland waterway. We may hope that the soul of Colles derived some solace that "in the great celebration which took place in [New York City] in November, 1825, when the waters of Erie united with

[13] New York State Assembly, *Journal*, Mar. 8, 1786, p. 76.
[14] DeWitt Clinton (pseudonym, Tacitus), "The services of Christopher Colles and of Jeffrey Smith," in David Hosack, *Memoir of DeWitt Clinton* (New York, 1829), Appendix, p. 283.
[15] Colles, *Proposals for Settlement*, p. 12.

the Atlantic, [his] effigy . . . was borne with appropriate dignity among the emblems of that vast procession." [16]

Failure to secure support for the Mohawk internal improvement project was undoubtedly one of the most disappointing in a succession of reverses experienced by the unfortunate Colles. Canals and waterways were his first and greatest love, and in the New York project he had envisioned great possibilities for the state and nation, and a means of gainful employment for himself. Some years passed, therefore, before he ventured again into this field.

Christopher Colles' last and most visionary waterway plan was set forth in a pamphlet published by him in 1808 and printed by Samuel Wood of New York. The impressive title reads *Proposal of a Design for the Promotion of the Interests of the United States of America, Extending its Advantages to All Ranks and Conditions of Men . . . by Means of Inland Navigable Communication of a New Construction and Mode* (Fig. 10). The plan called for the formation of two or more companies "who shall erect a number of *navigable canals*, not dug into the soil as in Europe, but built of timber entirely elevated above the ground. The sides of these canals to be perpendicular, so that goods may be loaded and unloaded the whole way." [17]

A canal constructed of timber, and above ground — this was a revolutionary idea. In Colles' justification for this new departure in canal building we sense some of the keen disappointment he felt at the failure of his earlier projects. "Ages and generations will pass away," he wrote, "before extensive dug canals can be completed in this country. This assertion cannot be controverted by the most strenuous advocates of the dug system, and many of the experiments and trials that have been made, seem to demonstrate it." [18]

Recognizing that it was "of much importance to pitch upon a convenient situation for the first experiment," Colles believed "that the route . . . from Middle-town Point to Burdentown or Burlington, will meet the approbation of the public, as it will be particularly to the cities of Philadelphia and New-York, and also to many of the inhabitants of New-Jersey." [19] The proposed canal was shown on an accom-

[16] Francis, "Reminiscences of Colles," p. 202.
[17] Colles, *Proposal of a Design*, p. 5.
[18] *Ibid.*, p. 4.
[19] *Ibid.*, p. 19.

# PROPOSAL OF A DESIGN

FOR

## THE PROMOTION OF

## *THE INTERESTS OF THE UNITED STATES OF AMERICA,*

EXTENDING ITS ADVANTAGES TO ALL RANKS AND
CONDITIONS OF MEN,

### WHETHER MONIED, LANDED, AGRICULTURAL, COMMERCIAL, MECHANICAL, OR MANUFACTURAL,

BY MEANS OF

## INLAND NAVIGABLE COMMUNICATIONS,

OF A NEW CONSTRUCTION AND MODE,

POSSESSING MANY ADVANTAGES SUPERIOR TO THE CANALS
EXECUTED IN EUROPE, MORE EXPEDITIOUSLY EXECUTED
AND CARRIED INTO IMMEDIATE OPERATION AND
EFFECT, COMPLETED AT A LESS EXPENSE, CON-
TAINING WITHIN ITSELF FUNDS AMPLY SUF-
FICIENT FOR FINISHING AND EXTENDING
IT TO ANY ASSIGNABLE DISTANCE, AND
EASILY KEPT IN REPAIR AND FULL
OPERATION FOR EVER.

———————

## BY CHRISTOPHER COLLES.

———————

### New-York :

## PRINTED FOR THE AUTHOR,

BY

## SAMUEL WOOD, NO. 362, PEARL-STREET.

..........

## 1808.

Fig. 10. Some of the assumed advantages of a timber canal are set forth
on the title page of this pamphlet, which introduced another Colles internal
improvement proposal. Courtesy of the Library of Congress.

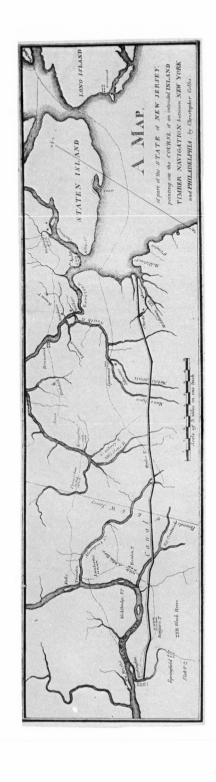

Fig. 11. The proposed timber canal across northern New Jersey is traced on this map by Christopher Colles. Courtesy of the Library of Congress.

panying *Map of Part of the State of New Jersey, Pointing out the Course of an Intended Inland Timber Navigation Between New York and Philadelphia,* by Christopher Colles (Fig. 11).

In an obvious effort to secure their support for the timber canal, Colles dedicated his *Proposal* "to the House Carpenters, Ship Carpenters, and Millwrights of the United States of America." He assured them that their "talents and labours can bring its execution into full operation and effect [and that] this design points out a new species of employment, exceedingly extensive and convenient for carpenters."

Colles also sought to obtain high level support for his project, and to this end sent a copy of the *Proposal* to President Thomas Jefferson. In his reply, sent from Washington, D. C., June 9, 1808, Jefferson wrote:

I thank you for the pamphlet containing your ideas on the subject of canals constructed of wood, but it is not in my power to give any opinion of its national importance. . . . It becomes the common question whether construction of wood, brick, or rough stone are the cheapest in the end? A question on which every man possesses materials for forming his judgment. I suspect it is the supposed necessity of using hewn stone in works of this kind which has had the greatest effect in discouraging their being undertaken. I tender you my salutations and respects.[20]

Salutations and respects, but once again there was no concrete support for patient and hopeful Christopher Colles. So burst the timber canal dream, as had so many of its predecessors.

[20] Thomas Jefferson, *Writings*, ed. Andrew A. Lipscomb (Washington, D. C., 1903), vol. 12, p. 74.

# V

# Colles During the Critical Years 1783-1789

His boundless energy and fertile mind rarely permitted Colles to concentrate on a single project or occupation. His multiple activity was also related to the economic needs of himself and his family. The November 23, 1785, petition to the New York City Council previously cited notes that he had established a dye factory which he proposed "to have carried on by his eldest son in case he shall be engaged in the prosecution of the navigation of the Mohawk River." [1]

Failure to obtain support for the Mohawk waterway project forced him to seek other means of subsistence. Thus we find a notice in the May 1, 1786, issue of the *New York Daily Advertiser* announcing "Electric Machines of a new construction exceeding portable and convenient and which will operate in the most unfavorable state of the weather, made by Christopher Colles at his Fig Blue manufactory the Lower battery." He further proposed "to exhibit a variety of entertaining experiments at his house on Tuesday, Thursday and Saturday at seven o'clock in the evening. Admittance two shillings." [2]

The "two shillings" earned from his public lectures were probably not overly abundant. They did, however, help feed the Colles family when other sources of income were lacking. The years from 1783 to 1790 were particularly lean ones for Colles, and lectures were often his only means of subsistence.

The talks covered a wide range of subjects in the fields of natural philosophy, mechanics, engineering, and military science. Colles knowledge of the latter, which helped him train some of the artillery officers of the Continental Army, was again called upon in the post war years. The Minutes of the New York Common Council for August 22, 1787, report that "a petition by Christopher Colles pray[s] the use

[1] Hall, "Early Pipe Line Projects," p. 702.
[2] *New York Daily Advertiser*, May 1, 1786.

of the Exchange Room for the purpose of giving Lectures on Gunnery &c was read and granted."

There is record too in 1789 of public lectures by the versatile engineer. A New York newspaper, in January of that year, carried an announcement "that so long as the sleighing lasted [Christopher Colles] would continue his electrical experiments and exhibitions of curiosities, at Halsey's celebrated tavern in Harlem."[3] Colles' resourcefulness is evident in thus capitalizing on the popular winter sport by presenting his lectures and exhibits at one of the taverns where sleighing parties stopped for warmth and refreshment. The interpretation of one writer, however, is that "it would seem from this that his lectures needed the incentive of a sleigh ride to make them more popular."[4]

The United States Constitution was adopted in 1787, and shortly thereafter the First Congress established import duties. John Lamb, who had been serving as Collector of Customs of the port of New York under an appointment of the State Legislature, was now named to the collectorship of the port by President Washington.

There was need in the Customs Office for a qualified person to test the specific gravity of imported spirits. To fill the position, Lamb called upon his old friend Christopher Colles. Finding his new office lacking in equipment of any kind, Colles, with characteristic ingenuity, designed and made his own proof glasses. It is improbable that the testing job occupied his full time, for there is evidence that he engaged in other activities during this period.

Through the years Colles' nimble mind conceived and devised a number of interesting and useful inventions. One such was the "solar microscope," which he described in a pamphlet published in 1815.[5] (Fig. 12) The instrument was actually designed some twenty-five years before this date, however. As early as August 1, 1789, a New York newspaper advertised an exhibit "at the house of Christopher Colles . . . every afternoon (provided the sun shines bright) of the Solar Microscope."[6]

[3] W. Harrison Bayles, *Old Taverns of New York* (New York, 1915), p. 366.
[4] *Ibid.*, p. 366.
[5] Christopher Colles, *An Account of the Astonishing Beauties and Operations of Nature . . . Displayed by the Solar Microscope* (New York, 1815).
[6] *New York Daily Advertiser*, Aug. 1, 1789.

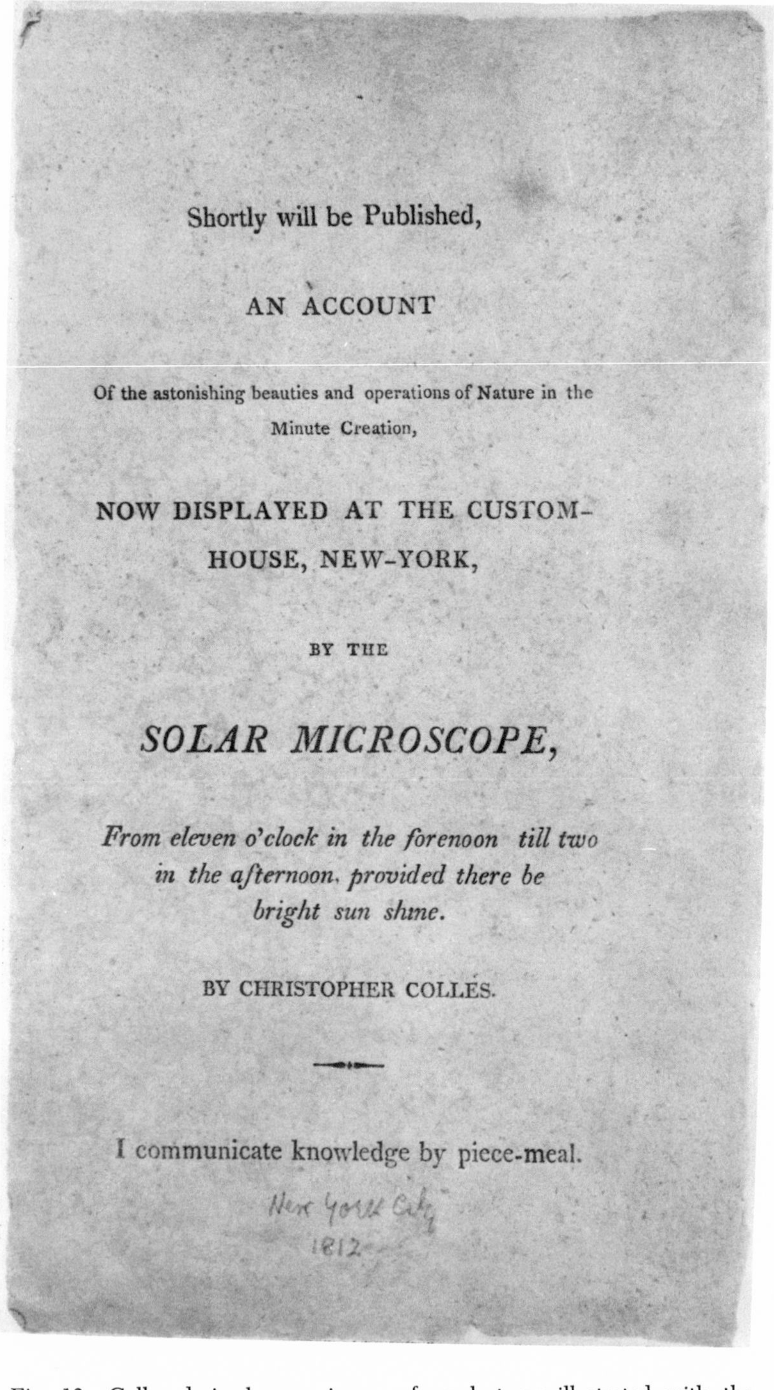

Shortly will be Published,

AN ACCOUNT

Of the astonishing beauties and operations of Nature in the
Minute Creation,

NOW DISPLAYED AT THE CUSTOM-
HOUSE, NEW-YORK,

BY THE

## SOLAR MICROSCOPE,

*From eleven o'clock in the forenoon till two
in the afternoon, provided there be
bright sun shine.*

BY CHRISTOPHER COLLES.

———•——

I communicate knowledge by piece-meal.

*New York City
1812*

Fig. 12. Colles derived some income from lectures illustrated with the
solar microscope, one of his many inventions. Courtesy of the New-York
Historical Society, New York City.

THE

# BEAUTIES OF NATURE,

## *EXHIBITED BY THE*

# *Solar Microscope.*

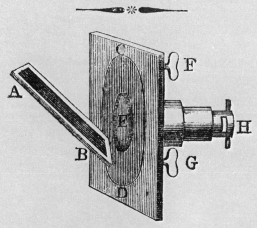

IN order to examine objects by the Solar Microscope, the room is made completely dark, and the sun's light being transmitted by the looking-glass **AB** through the lens **E** in a horizontal direction, the appearance of the object is thrown upon a white screen, or sheet, prodigiously magnified. In the fig-

Fig. 13. This diagram illustrates the operation of the solar microscope. Courtesy of the Library of Congress.

The microscope appears to have been a type of projection lantern, which utilized as a source of light the rays of the sun reflected from a mirror. The image of the object being viewed was projected, greatly enlarged, upon a white screen or sheet (Fig. 13). Among the interesting phenomena brought to public view by Colles' microscope were the eyes of insects, microscopic water life, blood cells, the leg of a spider, and enlargements of fleas and mites. In his booklet he noted that "the transparent membrane between the toes of a frog's hind foot, is an object very convenient for viewing the current and circulation of the blood; and in this, if well expanded, it may be seen fairly and distinctly, flowing through innumerable veins and arteries, like the rivers in a map." [7] The solar microscope, like his other inventions, did not add materially to Colles' income. He undoubtedly, however, derived considerable pleasure and satisfaction in revealing the wonders of nature to old and young alike. Perhaps, too, in the generation which followed, there were, among the distinguished and learned scientists, several who, as curious youngsters, received their first introduction to natural science through the solar microscope of Christopher Colles.

[7] Colles, *The Solar Microscope*, p. 5.

# VI

# The Survey of the Roads of the United States of America

Colles' preoccupation with cartography in the post-war years, and particularly from about 1787 to 1794, was probably inspired by surveying and mapping experiences during the Revolution. Definite data are lacking as to the exact nature of his cartographic contributions, and we can only conjecture as to how his skill was used by the Continental Army.

He was away from New York City, as has been reported, from late 1776 to the end of 1783. For portions of this period he is known to have been in Kingston, New York, and in Morristown, New Jersey. His forced migrations may have taken him, too, as far north as Albany. From here he may have made brief sorties into the Mohawk Valley. He certainly traveled through northern New Jersey, and may also have visited parts of eastern Pennsylvania and western Connecticut.

Colles' wartime wanderings were necessitated, in part at least, by the urgency of seeking refuge and earning a living for himself and his family during those trying and unsettled years. His natural restlessness undoubtedly also led him to wander afield and carry out personal investigations and studies whenever his time was not otherwise engaged.

Although apparently unfit for military duty Colles had, soon after his arrival in New York in 1774, cast his lot with the American patriots. John Lamb, one of his close friends, and an ardent leader of the Sons of Liberty, as has been seen, derived valuable information on military science and gunnery from Colles. There is reason to believe that Lamb, who became a successful artillery officer, may have assisted his scientific friend in securing employment during the war with the Artillery Department.

41

There is support for this assumption in Colles' letter to Washington of January 17, 1783, wherein he gives as personal references Gen. Henry Knox, Col. John Lamb, and Col. Alexander Hamilton, all of whom were, at one time or other, in the Artillery Department.

Knox, called the "father of the American Army Artillery," was an excellent organizer and a strict disciplinarian. While in winter quarters he established for his corps regular programs of study and training. Such a program was in effect during the terrible winter of 1777–1778 at Valley Forge, where Knox and his army were encamped. By the following spring "the artillery corps . . . for the first time reached a semblance of an integrated organization." [1]

At subsequent encampments, principally in New York and northern New Jersey, Knox's gunners were given further intensified training. So well did they learn their lessons that at Yorktown Lafayette remarked to Knox that "the progress of your artillery is . . . one of the wonders of the Revolution." [2] It is very probable that, with the recommendation and support of his good friend Col. Lamb, Colles may have assisted in educating and training Knox's artillery forces.

During the summers, when the Army was in the field, Colles may have employed his days conducting surveys and making maps. While so engaged, he looked ahead to the years of peace and reconstruction. One of the needs he envisioned for that happy day was a map of the new nation that traced its major transportation arteries.

Standard surveying instruments used during the Revolution, as well as in earlier years, were the compass and chain. The cumbersome, laborious process of measuring distances with the chain did not appeal to the impatient Colles. Accordingly, he put his inventive mind to work devising an instrument that would facilitate and speed this task. The result was the perambulator, which automatically recorded the revolution of a large wheel as it was propelled over the ground (Fig. 14).

Colles probably used his perambulator in road surveys during the war. The device apparently, however, required further adjustments and improvements. Several years after peace was reestablished we find him petitioning the United States Congress:

[1] North Callahan, *Henry Knox, General Washington's General* (New York, 1958), p. 133.
[2] *Ibid.*, p. 187.

Fig. 14. Perambulator of the type probably constructed by Colles and used in preparing maps for his *Survey of the Roads*. From legend on Map of County of Louth, in John Rocque's *Irish Surveys*, London [1760–1787]. Courtesy of the Library of Congress.

. . . that an exclusive privilege may be granted him in the benefits of an invention, which he has reduced to practice, for counting, with the utmost precision, the number of revolutions or vibrations of any wheel or other part of any mechanical engine or machine.[3]

There is no indication as to what action Congress took on the petition. The perambulator idea was not original with Colles, and similar devices had been used by surveyors long before his time. We may safely assume, therefore, that the request for "an exclusive privilege" was denied.

It is perhaps in keeping with the antithetical nature of Colles' career that he is best known today for his contributions to cartography, an interest that held his attention for a relatively brief period. To historians, bibliophiles, and cartographers, in particular, Colles is remembered primarily for his *Survey of the Roads of the United States of America, 1789.*

The *Survey*, in its most complete extant state, comprises a title page

[3] U. S. House of Representatives, *Journal, 1st and 2nd Congress*, I, 70 (Aug. 4, 1789).

# PROPOSALS

FOR PUBLISHING A

# SURVEY

OF THE

# ROADS

## Of the United States of America.

By CHRISTOPHER COLLES. *of New York*

## CONDITIONS.

1. THAT the work ſhall be neatly engraved upon copper, each page containing a delineation of near 12 miles of the road upon a ſcale of about one inch and three quarters to the mile, and particularly ſpecifying all the croſs roads and ſtreams of water which interſect it, the names of the moſt noted inhabitants of the houſes contiguous to or in view of the road ; the churches and other public buildings ; the taverns, blackſmith's ſhops, mills ~ d ~y opicᵗ ~ ~a ~c~ ~ render it a uſeful and entertaining work, and in ~ver~ f ~ct ~u ~he ſpecimen of the three firſt pages annexed.

2. That a ſet of general maps ſhall be made up~ .~ ~ll ſcale with references from them to the particular page where the deſcription of any road is to be found ; theſe maps will then anſwer as an index and will be found more convenient than any other index that can be made.

3. That each ſubſcriber ſhall pay one quarter dollar at the time of ſubſcribing (to defray ſeveral incidental charges neceſſary for the work) and one eighth of a dollar upon the delivery of every ſix pages of the work : but ſuch gentlemen as are willing to advance one dollar will be conſidered as patrons of the work, and will not be entitled to pay any more till the value thereof is delivered in.

4. That ſubſcribers ſhall pay 20 cents for each of the general maps and three cents for each ſheet of letter preſs in the alphabetical liſts or other neceſſary explanation of the drafts.

5. That each ſubſcriber ſhall be conſidered as engaging to take 100 pages.

6. That non-ſubſcribers ſhall pay three cents for each page of the work.

### Account of the advantages of theſe Surveys.

A traveller will here find ſo plain and circumſtantial a deſcription of the road, that whilſt he has the draft with him it will be impoſſible for him to miſs his way : he will have the ſatisfaction of knowing the names of many of the perſons who reſide on the road ; if his horſe ſhould want a ſhoe, or his carriage be broke, he will by the bare inſpection of the draft be able to determine whether he muſt go backward or forward to a blackſmith's ſhop : perſons who have houſes or plantations on the road may in caſe they want to let, leaſe, or ſell the ſame, advertiſe in the public newſpapers that the place is marked on ſuch a page of Colles's Survey of the roads ; this will give ſo particular a deſcription of its ſituation that no difficulty or doubt will remain about it. If a foreigner arrives in any part of the Continent and is under the neceſſity to travel by land, he applies to a bookſeller, who with the aſſiſtance of the index map chooſes out the particular pages which are neceſſary for his direction. It is expected many other entertaining and uſeful purpoſes will be diſcovered when theſe ſurveys come into general uſe.

*Subſcription papers will be ſent to moſt of the Bookſellers in the Continent*

Fig. 15. First state of the *Proposals* broadside. The manuscript additions, "of New York" and the sentence beginning "Subscription papers," were incorporated into the printed text of the second state. A paragraph testifying that "these surveys are made from actual mensuration," etc., was also added in the later edition. Courtesy of the New-York Historical Society, New York City.

and 83 small maps, which trace the major roads of the country from Albany, New York, on the north, and Stratford, Connecticut, on the northeast, southward to Yorktown and Williamsburg, Virginia. The maps are of the strip type, and two or three stretches of road are presented on each plate. There is no attempt to orient the maps on the page, and direction arrows are used to indicate north.

*Proposals for Publishing a Survey of the Roads*, a broadside first distributed in 1789, outlines in detail the plan for the road book (Fig. 15):

> The work [we read, was to] be neatly engraved upon copper, each page containing a delineation of near 12 miles of road upon a scale of about one inch and three quarters to the mile, and particularly specifying all the cross roads and streams of water which intersect it, the names of the most noted inhabitants of the houses contiguous to or in view of the road; the churches and other public buildings; the taverns, blacksmith's shops, mills, and every object which occurs to render it a useful and entertaining work.[4]

The road book was very probably conceived during the Revolution, and some of the surveys were undoubtedly made by Colles (with the aid of the perambulator) before the close of the war. The compilation of the first series of maps and the engraving of the plates and title page were accomplished quite likely between 1784 and 1789.

As set forth in the *Proposals*, the *Survey* was to be issued on a subscription basis, with each purchaser paying "one quarter dollar at the time of subscribing (to defray several incidental charges necessary for the work) and one eighth of a dollar upon the delivery of every six pages of the work."[5]

The first three plates, and very likely the title page, were distributed with the *Proposals* broadside. With plates 4, 5, 6, and 7, they map the road from New York City to Stratford, Connecticut. The title page, which is dated 1789, carries the engraving credit "C. Tiebout, Sculpt." Most bibliographers assume, therefore, that Tiebout also engraved the maps, although his name does not appear on any of them. It is possible, however, that his contribution to the road book was limited to engraving the title page and some of the earlier plates. Variations in style

---

[4] *Proposals for Publishing a Survey of the Roads of the United States of America by Christopher Colles of New York* (broadside).
[5] *Ibid.*

and symbols are apparent which may suggest that more than one engraver worked on the *Survey*. The symbol for mills, for example, is represented in the title page legend by a flared circle. Here and on a number of the earlier plates the lines radiating from the circle are rather generously applied. On most of the later maps and on some of the early ones, the radiating lines are limited to eight or nine, and are more regularly distributed. Differences in style of lettering may also be discerned. A fine, somewhat ornate, italic or cursive style is used on certain of the early maps and on a number of the southern ones (for example, Head Lynch, pl. 72; Dillion, pl. 76; Burntbrick Ord$^y$, pl. 77; Port Royal, pl. 85; Lindsey, pl. 85).

There are also inconsistencies in the use of the tavern symbol. On most of the maps the symbol is placed approximately at right angles to the bottom of the page. On a few of the early plates (for example, pls. 3, 4, 5) some tavern symbols are oriented instead with the direction of the road, and may even be upside down with relation to the reader (for example, Nichol's tavern, pl. 7, and Van Wyck's, pl. 12). The arm of the tavern sign points to the right quite consistently on the lower numbered plates. Beginning with plate 13, however, the arm of the symbol points, apparently with no reason, either to the right or the left.

While these differences in style and practice may represent the experiments of a single person, we cannot eliminate the possibility that Tiebout did not engrave all the *Survey* plates.

Cornelius Tiebout, a native of New York, is one of the first American-born engravers. A map of New York City, engraved by him, was published in the 1789 New York City Directory (Fig. 16). Between 1789 and 1793 he engraved landscape scenes and several maps for New York magazines (Fig. 17), and in the latter year went to London for further study. There, under James Heath, Tiebout mastered a stipple technique that he employed on a series of portraits, first in New York City and after 1799 in Philadelphia.[6] The work he did for Colles' survey is among the earliest engraving done by Tiebout and is not recorded in Stauffer's catalog.

We may wonder how Colles came to engage the young and inex-

[6] David M. Stauffer, *American Engravers Upon Copper and Steel* (New York, 1907), I, 271–272.

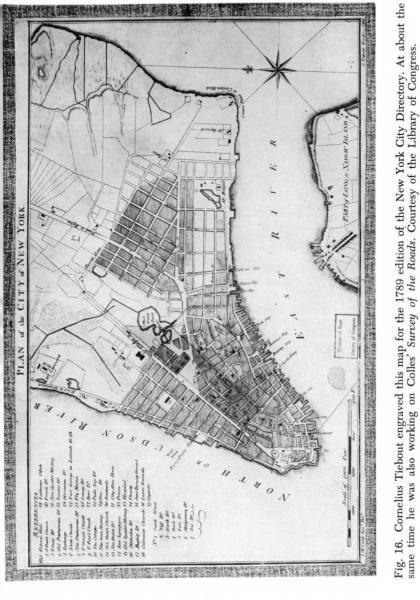

Fig. 16. Cornelius Tiebout engraved this map for the 1789 edition of the New York City Directory. At about the same time he was also working on Colles' *Survey of the Roads.* Courtesy of the Library of Congress.

Fig. 17. This view of the Falls on the Schuylkill River was engraved by Cornelius Tiebout shortly before he left America for study in London. From *New York Magazine*, May 1793. Courtesy of the Library of Congress.

perienced Tiebout as his engraver. In his chronic impecunious state, he was probably not able to employ a more experienced craftsman. Cornelius Tiebout was one of several sons born in New York City to Tunis and Elizabeth Lamb Tiebout. It is possible that Tiebout's mother and Christopher Colles' good friend, Col. John Lamb, were related, and that the latter was the contact between the *Survey's* map maker and engraver.

Stauffer gives 1777 as the supposed birth date of Tiebout. This is obviously incorrect, for he would have been only 12 years old in 1789, the year when the title page for Colles' road book was engraved. Tiebout's parents were married about 1750, and Cornelius (who had several older brothers and sisters) was more probably born around 1760.

There is a possibility that Cornelius was in military service during the Revolution. In the *History of Schoharie County*, Simms includes a "Cornelius Teabout" in a scouting party for Col. William Butler's 4th Pennsylvania Regiment in April 1780. At the time Butler's army was participating in General Sullivan's punitive expedition against the Indians and Tories in upper New York State.[7] If the "Cornelius Teabout" of Butler's Regiment was really Cornelius Tiebout of New York, he may also have been a source for some of the geographical data on which Colles based his New York waterway proposal.

As set forth in the *Proposals*, the *Survey of the Roads* was published on a subscription basis. This was a common practice of the time and particularly appealed to Colles, who lacked capital to complete the entire work before releasing it. The purchase terms and price were quite reasonable. Each subscriber was to:

. . . pay one quarter dollar at the time of subscribing (to defray several incidental charges necessary for the work) and one eighth of a dollar upon the delivery of every six pages of the work: but such gentlemen as are willing to advance one dollar will be considered as patrons of the work, and will not be entitled to pay any more till the value thereof is delivered in.[8]

The cost per individual page was 20 cents, and each subscriber was "considered as engaging to take 100 pages." [9]

The title page of the *Survey* bears the date 1789, and most authorities have accepted this as the year of publication. Colles undoubtedly had hoped to issue the first series of plates in that year, and the title page no doubt was engraved in 1789. It may have been early in 1790, however, before subscribers received their first set of road maps.

Advance subscriptions resulting from the *Proposals* leaflet apparently were not numerous. Colles, therefore, sought to enlist the aid of printers and booksellers to market his road guide. Some extant copies of the leaflet carry a manuscript note reading "Subscription papers will be sent to most of the Booksellers on the continent." (See Fig. 15.) This line appears in print on an obviously later issue of the broadside.

A few printers were interested. Thus we read in the March 10, 1790, issue of the *Freeman's Journal* (Philadelphia) that there is "Now Publishing at New York, and to be Sold by the Printer hereof, A Survey of the Roads of the United States of America Made from actual mensuration." [10] The advertisement was carried in the paper sporadically

---

[7] Jeptha R. Simms, *History of Schoharie County and the Border Wars of New York* (Albany, 1845), p. 325.
[8] Colles, *Proposals for Publishing.*
[9] *Ibid.*
[10] *The Freeman's Journal*, or *North American Intelligencer*, March 10, 1790.

for the next seven months, with the last appearance on October 6. Although a search through other contemporary newspapers disclosed no similar notices, it is possible that additional announcements were printed.

The costs of preparing and launching the road guide severely taxed the meager resources of Christopher Colles, and returns from subscriptions and sales hardly sufficed to finance additional plates. The enterprising map maker, therefore, sought help from the New York State Legislature. Accordingly, in the State Assembly, on March 13, 1790, "a petition of Christopher Colles, praying aid of the Legislature to enable him to proceed in an intended survey of roads, by means of a perambulator, was read and referred to Mr. J. Brown, Mr. Havens, and Mr. Clowes." [11]

Several days later the Committee "reported, that as the object for the attainment whereof the petitioner prays aid of the Legislature, are by him considered and intended to be of national utility, it would in the opinion of the committee be most proper for him to make application to the general government for support of his business, and therefore that the prayer of the petition ought not to be granted." [12] The Assembly concurred with the recommendation of its committee.

Colles, desperately in need of aid to further his *Survey*, hastened to make his plea to the Congress of the United States. On March 30, 1790, his petition "was presented to the House and read, praying to be employed by Congress in a survey and publication of the Roads of the United States." [13] The petition was referred to the Postmaster General, who, charged with distributing the mail, had a real interest in transportation problems of the young republic. Samuel Osgood, head of the Post Office Department, seriously considered Colles' request, and submitted a favorable report on it.

His letter, communicated to the House of Representatives on April 27, 1790, follows:

The Postmaster General to whom was referred the memorial of Christopher Colles, with orders to examine and report his opinion on same, begs leave to submit the following observations: The General Post Office is subject to

[11] New York State Assembly, *Journal*, March 13, 1790.
[12] *Ibid.*, March 16, 1790.
[13] U. S. House of Representatives, *Journal, 1st & 2nd Congress*, I, 185 (March 30, 1790).

many inconveniences for the want of a survey and map of the roads of the United States. The obtaining of same will be of great public as well as private utility. The objections that may be made against the plan of the memorialist will naturally arise from a supposed inaccuracy in the execution — the measurement of the roads by a perambulator not being so much to be relied on as by a chain, and that the extensiveness of the work will exceed the ability of the memorialist.

From the experiments that have been made by the memorialist, the measurement appears to be accurate for the establishing of distances on the post roads: as, in a distance of ten miles, there was only a variation of ten feet, and in ninety miles an exact agreement with the measurement made by the chain. When the roads are very uneven and broken, the perambulator will make the distance greater, in proportion to the unevenness of the surface than it would be by measuring with a chain. The experiments, however, that have been made, were upon roads that were as uneven as the roads are, in a general view, in the United States. The ability of the memorialist to execute the work within a reasonable time is evident from what he has already executed, and as it is the principal, if not the only dependence he has for the support of himself and his family, there is no doubt but he will be as in·lustrious as his slender means will permit.

The assistance requested of the public, at the rate of one eighth of a dollar ɟ ɘr mile, will amount to about three hundred and seventy-five dollars: for ˙ne extent to be surveyed cannot vary much from three thousand miles. The Postmaster General, upon a due consideration of the benefits that will result from the execution of the work undertaken by the memorialist, is of the opinion that the public interest will be promoted by granting him the aid prayed for, in proportion to the distance surveyed, and the publication, after being qualified to its having been done with proper attention.

All of which is respectfully submitted<br>[signed] Samuel Osgood.[14]

The Postmaster General's report was read in the House on April 27, 1790, but despite its favorable recommendation was "ordered to lie on the table."

A month later the *Journal* of the House of Representatives noted that it was "Ordered that the report of the Postmaster General, on the petition of Christopher Colles, be referred to the committee, to whom was re-committed the bill for regulating the Post Office of the

---

[14] *American State Papers, Class VIII, Post Office Department, Documents Legislative and Executive of the Congress of the United States 1789 to 1833* (Washington, 1834), p. 3. The original manuscript letter is in the U. S. National Archives.

United States, with instructions to insert a clause or clauses pursuant to the said report." [15]

The young Congress was confronted with too many problems and with more pressing demands upon the nation's financial resources to give serious consideration to roads or road maps. Consequently no action was taken on the recommendation of the Postmaster General. Once again Christopher Colles' hopes were quashed and he was forced to seek aid in other quarters to proceed with his *Survey*.

Osgood's letter is one of the best sources of information on the nature and character of Colles' road project. His estimate of 3000 miles of surveys is somewhat greater than the estimate originally given by Colles in his *Proposals*. In the latter, subscribers were "considered as engaging to take 100 pages." With each map covering some 12 miles of road, the complete survey would have included approximately 1200 miles of highways. Actually only 83 plates were published, covering slightly less than 1000 miles.

The cost of "⅛ dollar per mile" seems ridiculously low, and we may wonder how Colles hoped to make a profit. The perambulator did, of course, permit a fairly rapid traverse, and there was the additional income from subscribers. Nevertheless, even had Congress granted the aid requested, the project might have proved to be financially unprofitable.

Despite the failure of Congress to supply the requested aid, Colles somehow managed to continue for a time with the *Survey*. We can only conjecture as to how he was able to compile and publish the 83 plates included in the most complete known copies of the road book. The plates are numbered consecutively from 1 to 86, with numbers 45, 46, and 47 duplicated and identified with asterisks. Plates 34 to 39 are lacking, indicating that the road guide as published fell short of the goal set by its compiler. We do not know exactly when the last of the published plates were distributed. The project was, however, probably abandoned in late 1791 or early 1792.

[15] U. S. House of Representatives, *Journal*, p. 228 (May 31, 1790).

# VII

# Source Materials Used in Compiling
# the Road Book

THE road map project was certainly original with Colles and was probably planned during the war when he became acutely aware of the lack of good transportation maps. As has been observed, some of his efforts while the Revolution was in progress were directed toward inventing a perambulator with which he made surveys of the roads in the several regions where he had temporary residence.

His wartime travels were primarily in New York State, but he also is known to have lived in New Jersey and may possibly have spent brief periods in eastern Pennsylvania and western Connecticut. There is no evidence that Colles ever traveled farther south than the Philadelphia area. Where then did he obtain detailed data for the maps in the *Survey* that show the southern part of the country?

The late Lawrence Martin, former Chief of the Library of Congress Map Division, cast the first light on this problem almost a quarter of a century ago. In his *Annual Report* to the Librarian of Congress, for the fiscal year 1937, Martin stated:

We learned that the printed maps in Christopher Colles's road book. . . which show the ancient road from Georgetown to Alexandria . . . were made in 1781 by Simeon DeWitt at the direction of George Washington. DeWitt's manuscript maps . . . were dated through finding in the Rutgers University Library and in our own Division of Manuscripts letters of August 29 and November 4, 1781, in which George Washington directed DeWitt to survey this and other roads on his way from Brunswick, N. J. to Yorktown, Va. . . . Colles's printed maps contain nothing which is not on DeWitt's.

Martin, therefore, concluded "that Colles made none of the maps heretofore attributed to him as author." [1]

[1] Lawrence Martin, "Division of Maps," in *U. S. Library of Congress: Annual*

Griffin, writing more recently, is less harsh. He observes that:

While Colles had undoubtedly accomplished considerable personal measurement of areas of New York and New Jersey, it is doubtful that the southern portions of the route are the result of his own calculations. His precarious financial status would have made extensive travel impractical if not impossible. Much of his data seems to have been obtained from the road surveys of Robert Erskine and Simeon DeWitt, military geographers and successive surveyors-general, made for the Continental Army at the order of Washington.[2]

This conclusion seems to be more in accord with available evidence than is Martin's.

Plates 51 to 86 in Colles' *Survey* map the roads from Philadelphia south to Williamsburg and Yorktown, Virginia. A comparison of these plates with the corresponding DeWitt maps reveals almost identical names and features on both. Note, for example, the similarity in names on Erskine-DeWitt Map 124–M and plates 65 and 66 in Colles' *Survey* (Fig. 18):

| *Erskine-DeWitt Map 124–M* | *Colles Plates 65 & 66* |
|---|---|
| Patowmack River | Potowmack R[r] |
| Alexandria | Alexandria |
| Dan[l] McCallister | McAllister |
| To Loudon County | to Loudon County |
| Great Hunting Creek | [Creek shown, but not named] |
| Ben Delany, Esq. | Delany Esq. |
| Gen[l] Washington's Land | Gen. Washington's Land |
| old road | Old Road |
| Accohick Creek | Accohick Cr. |
| Pohick Church | Pohick Church |
| To Pohick Warehouse | to Pohick Warehouse |
| To Newgate | to Newgate |
| To Pasys Ferry | to Pasy's ferry |
| Boggs | Boggs |

The parallelism of data on the two series of maps is so close that there

*Report for the Fiscal Year Ending June 30, 1937.* Typescript copy in Library of Congress Map Division.

[2] Lloyd W. Griffin, "Christopher Colles and His Two American Map Series," *Bibliographical Society of America: Papers*, vol. 48 (1954), p. 175.

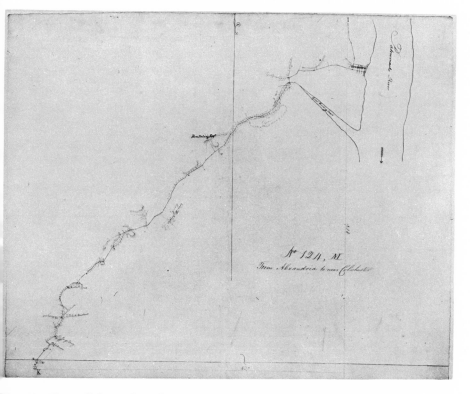

Fig. 18. The road from Alexandria south to near Colchester, Virginia, is mapped on No. 124–M of the Erskine-DeWitt series. The information shown on Colles Plates 65 & 66 was almost certainly derived from this map. Courtesy of the New-York Historical Society, New York City.

can be little doubt that Colles used the surveys of Washington's geographers as the primary source for his plates 51 to 86.

Roads crossing New Jersey, between New York and Philadelphia, are presented on plates 40 to 50, including the three extra ones numbered 45*, 46*, and 47*. Portions of this region Colles knew personally, both from his early residence in Philadelphia and from possible travels in New Jersey during the Revolution. We might expect, therefore, that the maps for these roads would be based on Colles' own surveys. This is not the case, however, for the information on these plates also matches very closely that found on the New Jersey military surveys of Erskine and DeWitt.

The striking parallelism is evident in the following sequence of names between Brunswick and Princeton on Erskine-DeWitt Map 121–A and Colles' plates 43 and 44 (Fig. 19):

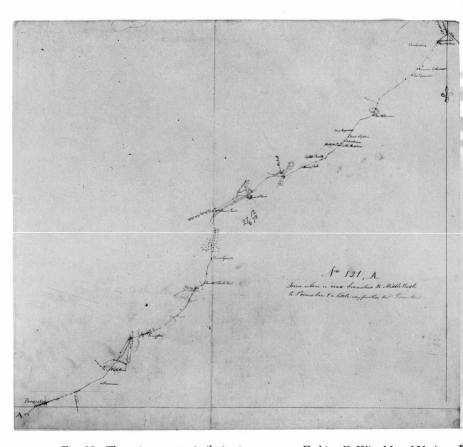

Fig. 19. There is a great similarity in names on Erskine-DeWitt Map 121–A and Colles Plates 43 & 44, which show the road extending northeast from Princeton, New Jersey. Courtesy of the New-York Historical Society, New York City.

| Erskine-DeWitt Map 121–A | Colles Plates 43 & 44 |
|---|---|
| To Brunswick | Brunswick |
| To Middlebush & Somerset | to Middlebush & Somerset |
| Clawsons Tav[n] | Clawson's [tavern] |
| John Waldron | Waldron |
| Van Leva's | Van Leva |
| Hermann Cortleyaws | Cotleyaw |
| Sam[l] Garrison | Garrison |
| Sam[l] Williamson | Williamson |
| Ben. Hageman | Hageman |
| James Sydam | Sydam |
| Schoolhouse | |
| Whitlocks Tav[n] or the Hudibras | Whitlock at Hudibras [tavern] |

| | |
|---|---|
| Dutch Church | Dutch Church |
| Henry Cock | Cock |
| Cobin Wykoff | Wykoff |
| Isaac Sleover | Slover |
| Wm Jones's Tavn | Jones [tavern] |
| To Rocky Hill Mills | to Rocky hill mills |
| David Gano's | Gano |
| Barthw Fort's Tavn | Fort's [tavern] |
| Rocky Hill | Rocky Hill |
| Kingston | Kingston |
| Millstone River | Millstone Rr |
| Harry's Brook | Harry's brook |
| White House | White house |
| Gate road | Gate road |
| Furmans | Furman |
| To Allentown | to Allentown |
| Princeton | Jug-town |
| | Princeton |

*Survey* plates 1 to 33 trace roads between New York City and Albany, New York City and Stratford, Connecticut, Stratford to Poughkeepsie, and Albany to Newburgh, N. Y., along the west side of the Hudson River. It is this part of the road book that invalidates Martin's contention "that Colles made none of the maps heretofore attributed to him."[3] Such similarity as there is between the Colles and Erskine-DeWitt maps for these regions is no more than one might reasonably expect from two independent surveys of the same area. Moreover, there are among the extant Erskine-DeWitt maps, none which are identical in area and data with Colles' plates 1 to 33. Note, for example, the large number of names, for the stretch of road extending south from Peekskill, on Colles' plates 10 and 11, only a few of which are shown on Erskine-DeWitt Map 32, for the corresponding region.

| *Erskine-DeWitt Map 32* | *Colles Plates 10 & 11* |
|---|---|
| Peekskill | Peekskill |
| | Dusenburys [tavern] |
| | to Crumpond |
| | Lt. Govr Cortlandt |

[3] Martin, *Annual Report.*

57

| | |
|---|---|
| Hercules Fort | Wattles (blacksmith) |
| | to Mill |
| | P. Haws Esq$^r$ |
| | Forsyth |
| | De Pue |
| | Birdsalls [tavern] |
| | to Peeks Kill Land$^g$ |
| | Grifins [blacksmith] |
| | to Crumpond |
| T. Barkot | Vermilyea |
| | Cronk |
| | Van Tassel |
| | Lent |
| | Lents [tavern] |
| | Merk |
| | Conklin |
| Captain Lilly | Cap Lilly |
| | Lent [blacksmith] |
| Calebergh | Haight |
| | Goetchins |
| | Mason |
| | to River |
| Abraham Wierst | Hartshorn |
| | Chatherton |
| | Fine view of N. River |
| | Hammond |
| | Tuttle |
| Fn$^o$ Barret | Barret |
| | Dijckman |
| | Haynes |
| | to River |
| | Merrits [tavern] |
| | to Crum pond |

Colles is believed to have spent most of his wartime exile from New York City in the Hudson highlands. It was here very likely that he devised and perfected the perambulator and utilized it for his surveys. The roads on both sides of the Hudson were probably surveyed during the Revolution. The road from New York City to Poughkeepsie, via Stratford, Connecticut, may have been surveyed in 1789 to prove for the benefit of the legislators from whom Colles sought assistance that such surveys could be made accurately with the perambulator. It will be recalled that in his April 27, 1790, report to Congress on Colles' petition, the Postmaster General referred to an experimental survey of ninety miles which had been made.

Plates 34 to 39 are not found in any extant copy of Colles' *Survey of the Roads*, and it is generally assumed that they were never issued. Church believed that these numbers "may have been reserved for a map of the roads from Newburgh to New York along the west bank of the Hudson." [4] This seems to be a logical supposition, for there is in that section the only break in the overall continuity of roads shown in the *Survey*. The absence of these pages lends further support to the belief that Colles personally carried out the surveys on which the first thirty-three plates were based.

The sequence of events that produced the *Survey of the Roads of the United States* may be reconstructed as follows. During the Revolution Colles probably surveyed and mapped the roads between Poughkeepsie and Albany, and from Albany to Newburgh. This data was later incorporated on plates 14, 21 to 25, and 26 to 33 of the *Survey*. It is possible that these surveys were made for the Continental Army although, as previously noted, no record of Colles' military employment has been found.

The stretch of road between Poughkeepsie and New York was very likely surveyed after the British departed and Colles returned to the city. By this time compilation of the road book was proving to be a bigger task than the enterprising map maker had anticipated. Consequently in 1790 he sought help, first of the New York Legislature and then from the United States Congress. As evidence of his ability to complete the project successfully, he surveyed the roads from New York to Stratford, Connecticut, and from Stratford to Poughkeepsie.

[4] Elihu D. Church, *A Catalogue of Books Relating to the Discovery and Early History of North and South America*, ed. G. W. Cole (New York, 1951), vol. 5, p. 1789.

After his request for assistance was turned down by both the New York Legislature and the United States Congress, Colles apparently sought some inexpensive means of completing the *Survey* and fulfilling his commitment to subscribers.

In some manner he managed to secure copies of the surveys made by Washington's military geographers, and from these he compiled maps for the region south of New York. Because he hoped later to complete maps for the road south of Newburgh, Colles reserved numbers 34 to 39 for these prospective plates. Accordingly, the first map, based on the military surveys, is numbered 40.

The similarity of data on the two map series suggests that Colles relied primarily upon the Erskine-DeWitt maps for his last 50 plates. Inasmuch as the data were used with only minor editorial changes, compilation and engraving of these plates probably was accomplished quite rapidly and may have been completed by 1791 or 1792.

If Cornelius Tiebout engraved all the plates, the job would have had to be done no later than 1792, for the following year the young engraver went to London for further study.

It is possible, however, that Colles' daughter Eliza engraved some of the plates. Lossing, in his *History of New York City*, states that "Colles constructed and published a series of sectional road maps, which were engraved by his daughter." [5] There is supporting evidence for Lossing's statement in the credit line "Eliza Colles, Sculp." that appears on two of the plates in the *Geographical Ledger*, a subsequent cartographic project of the versatile Colles.

Some differences in style and technique, as mentioned previously, may be noted between the early and later plates. Whether these variations indicate that more than one craftsman prepared the *Survey* plates or represent modifications by a single engraver as the project progressed we cannot be certain.

There can be little doubt, however, that the surveys of Washington's military geographers were the prime compilation source for more than half the maps in Colles' *Survey of the Roads of the United States*. The question remains, however, as to how the misfortune-dogged engineer secured the official Revolutionary War maps. The story of these

[5] Benson Lossing, *History of New York City* (New York, 1884), p. 75.

maps has never been told in detail, and a word about them may, therefore, be pertinent here.

The mapping of the Atlantic seaboard had of course been initiated by the first adventurers who touched these shores in the sixteenth century. With establishment of colonies at various points along the coast early in the seventeenth century, land surveys were made to determine boundaries of grants and property. Some venturesome individuals dared to explore the wild interior country and drew crude maps of the regions they visited.

As many of these fragmentary surveys as they could secure were used by commercial cartographers to supply the demands of map-hungry Europeans. Most printed maps, before the Revolution, were prepared and distributed by publishers in England and on the continent. While virtually every colonial settlement had one or more surveyors, map making as a profession did not become established in America until after the Revolution.

Units of the British Army were retained in various parts of the colonies before the Revolution. Topographical engineers had prepared a number of military maps that were put to good use by British commanders during the war.

The Continental Army was less well supplied cartographically when the Revolution began. As Douglas Southall Freeman has noted, "In 1775, Washington could procure such maps only as had been engraved for a small, discouraging market. When he went into an unmapped area, he found few natives who knew anything more than the direction of the roads and the course of the streams immediately at hand." [6]

Washington was not one to tolerate for long a lack of maps. In a letter to the President of Congress, written from his Morristown headquarters on January 26, 1777, he complained that:

. . . The want of accurate Maps of the Country which has hitherto been the Scene of the War, has been a great disadvantage to me. I have in vain endeavored to procure them, and have been obliged to make shift, with such Sketches, as I could trace out from my own Observations and that of Gentlemen around me.

[6] Douglas S. Freeman, *George Washington, a Biography*, vol. 5 (New York, 1952), p. 169a.

61

He went on to propose that "if Gentlemen of known Character and probity, could be employed in making Maps (from actual Survey) of the Roads, Rivers, Bridges and Fords over them, the mountains and passes thro' them, it would be of the Greatest Advantage." [7]

The General underlined the need in a letter, dated July 19, 1777, addressed jointly to Philip Livingston, Elbridge Gerry, and George Clymer, influential members of the Continental Congress.

A Good Geographer [he wrote] to Survey the Roads and take Sketches of the Country where the Army is to Act would be extremely useful and might be attended with exceeding valuable consequences. He might with propriety have the chief direction of the Guides who must have a head to procure, govern, and pay them. If such a person should be approved of I would beg leave to recommend Mr. Robt. Erskine who is thoroughly skilled in this business, has already assisted us in making maps of the country, and has (as I am informed) uniformly supported the Character of a fast friend to America.[8]

The Congress approved Washington's recommendation, and on July 27, 1777, Robert Erskine was commissioned Geographer and Surveyor-General to the Continental Army. Erskine, who was born in Scotland in 1735, was trained as a hydraulic engineer. After periods of employment in his native country and in England, he emigrated to America in 1771 to take over the management of an iron making establishment in New Jersey, owned by a group of British investors. Although conscientiously handling the affairs of his absentee employers, Erskine was deeply sympathetic with the cause of the colonists. When the Revolution broke out, therefore, he cast his lot with the patriots.

Erskine was well qualified for the task for which Washington selected him. In a letter to the Commander-in-Chief, dated August 1, 1777, he outlined some of the problems he envisioned and how they might be solved.

In planning a country [he explained] a great part of the ground must be walked over, particularly the banks of Rivers and Roads; as much of which may be traced and laid down in three hours as could be walked over in one;

[7] George Washington, *Writings*, ed. John C. Fitzpatrick (Washington, 1931–1944), VII, 65.
[8] *Ibid.*, VII, 443.

or in other words a Surveyor who can walk 15 miles a day may plan 5 miles
. . . six attendants to each surveyor will be proper; to wit, two chain-bearers,
one to carry the instrument, and three to hold flag staffs. . . . Young gentlemen of Mathematical genius, who are acquainted with the principles of
Geometry, and who have a taste for drawing would be the most proper
assistants for a Geographer.[9]

One qualified "young gentleman" was Simeon DeWitt, who joined
Erskine's staff as Assistant Geographer in 1778. Born in Ulster County,
New York, on December 25, 1756, DeWitt had shortly before graduated
from Queens (now Rutgers) University, and had participated as a
volunteer in the brief campaign against General Burgoyne. Simeon
was the nephew of General James Clinton, who recommended him to
Washington for appointment to the Geographer's staff.

Erskine, with some assistants, began surveys toward the end of 1777,
apparently in the region bordering the Hudson River. In April 1778,
Washington wrote to him: "I received yours of the 26th, March, in-
closing an elegant draft of part of Hudson's River. If your affairs are
in such a situation that they will admit of your attendance upon the
Army I shall be glad to see you as soon as possible." [10]

Surveyors were still operating in that area several months later, for
on July 31, 1778, Washington directed General James Clinton to move
"with the detachment under your command . . . towards Kings Bridge
and the Enemy's lines thereabouts. The principal objects in view are,
to cover the Engineers and Surveyors, while they reconnoiter and
as far as time will permit, survey the grounds & roads in your rear,
and in front of the Camp." [11]

Erskine and DeWitt were assisted in their mapping activities by
a number of other surveyors. The names of only a few of these assistants are known to us, however. The Sullivan Expedition, sent through
Pennsylvania and into upper New York State, in 1778 and 1779, to
subdue the marauding Indians and Tories in those regions, was accompanied by several members of the Geographer's Department.
Capt. William Gray and Lt. Benjamin Lodge were attached to Col.
William Butler's Fourth Pennsylvania Regiment. They surveyed and

[9] In George Washington, *Papers*, MS., Library of Congress Manuscript Division.
[10] Washington, *Writings*, ed. Fitzpatrick, XI, 246.
[11] George Washington, *Letters to George and James Clinton* (New York, [1934]), p. 29.

mapped the route of the army from Easton, across the mountains to Wyoming, Pennsylvania, along the Susquehanna River between Sunbury and Wyoming, and north to the Genesee River in New York State. A number of the drafts, prepared on the Expedition, are among the extant Erskine-DeWitt maps.[12]

In early 1779 Erskine was established in headquarters at his estate Ringwood in northern New Jersey near the New York State line. Washington was concerned over the safety of this location and wrote on March 3, 1779, "I can assure you, your work is no secret [to the enemy]. Some of the Convention officers who were at your House, saw the Maps and mentioned the accuracy and great Value of them." [13]

During the Revolution there were no facilities for rapid reproduction or duplication of maps. From the surveyor's rough field notes a finished map was prepared by draftsmen. If extra copies were desired, they were laboriously traced by hand from the original. Maps were consequently scarce and were supplied only to the highest field commanders.

For reasons of security, too, the number of maps was limited, as is indicated in Erskine's letter of July 3, 1779, to Baron von Steuben. "I beg leave," he wrote, "to transmit you the enclosed Draught of the Adjacent Country — at the same time His Exy. [i.e., Washington] desired me to mention it as His particular request that no Copies whatever be permitted to be taken of it." [14]

Washington, with his background in surveying, relied greatly upon the maps prepared by Erskine and his staff. Thus early in August 1779 he asked in a letter sent from his West Point headquarters, "Are the cross roads between the Sussex and Morristown Roads Surveyed? If they are I wish to have them laid down on my pocket Map as soon as possible; If they are not, no time should be lost in the completion of this necessary work." [15]

The same letter directs Erskine, "If you have any Assistant with you, unimployed, he may Survey the Road from Stamford to Hartford

[12] New York State, Secretary of State, *Journals of the Military Expedition of Major General John Sullivan* (Auburn, N. Y., 1887).

[13] Washington, *Writings*, ed. Fitzpatrick, XIV, 182–183.

[14] Albert H. Heusser, *The Forgotten General, Robert Erskine* (Paterson, N. J., 1928), p. 154.

[15] Washington, *Writings*, ed. Fitzpatrick, XVI, 60.

by the way of Norwalk Fairfield and New Haven and come back the most direct Public Road from New Haven to Bedford." [16]

Erskine's untimely death on October 2, 1780, at the age of 45, was a serious blow to the mapping program of the Continental Army. Fortunately, he had a competent young assistant, and on December 4, 1780, Simeon DeWitt was appointed Geographer-in-Chief.

Some eight months earlier, in a letter to Gen. Philip Schuyler, Erskine had summarized the map work accomplished by his department up to that time:

From Surveys actually made, we have furnished His Excellency with maps of both sides of the North River, extending from New Windsor and Fishkill, southerly to New York; eastward to Hartford, Whitehaven, etc. and on the west to Easton in Pennsylvania. Our Surveys likewise include the principal part of New Jersey, lying northward of a line drawn from Sandy Hook to Philadelphia; take in a considerable part of Pennsylvania; extend through the whole route of the Western Army under Genl. Sullivan; and are carried on from New Windsor and Fishkill northward, on both sides of the River, to Albany, and from thence to Scoharie. In short, from the Surveys made, and materials collecting and already procured, I could form a pretty accurate Map of the four States of Pennsylvania, New Jersey, New York and Connecticut, and by the help of a few magnetic and Astronomical Observations, with some additional Surveys, a very accurate one.[17]

Erskine's reference to the mapping of both sides of the Hudson is of interest to the Colles story. Detailed surveys of all of this region are not included in the Erskine-DeWitt maps now in the collections of the New-York Historical Society. Furthermore, except for the early months of the war, when Erskine and his assistants conducted some surveys in the lower valley, there is no record that Washington's geographers mapped the Hudson River region.

Colles, we know, was in the Hudson River area early in the war. Despite the absence of any official records, was he at the time serving in the Geographer's Department? Or, as indicated previously, were the Hudson valley maps prepared for another branch of the Continental Army, most likely the Artillery Department? If the latter, Erskine and his staff obviously were informed about these surveys, as indicated in the letter to General Schuyler.

[16] *Ibid.*
[17] Heusser, *The Forgotten General*, p. 165.

DeWitt joined Washington at New Windsor, New York, on December 16, 1780, and remained with the headquarters of the army until the close of the war. The following February, in a letter to Col. Timothy Pickering, Washington notes that the road from New Windsor, via White House, Germantown, and Warwick, "I am informed is the nearest and best to Trenton [and] Mr. DeWit is now about measuring of it." [18]

Surveying and mapping during the Revolution were largely of a reconnaissance character, with no common base of reference. It was, consequently, difficult to combine the several surveys into a coordinated map. In an attempt to solve this problem, in part at least, we find DeWitt advertising in August 1781 that

> Any Mathematical Gentleman who can furnish the subscriber with the correct variation of the needle in any places in Connecticut, New-York, New Jersey and Pennsylvania, shall have their services gratefully acknowledged; as many observations of this kind as can be collected will be of use in perfecting maps formed of those parts of the country, for His excellency General Washington. N.B. It will be necessary to mention the times and names of the places (also their latitude if ascertained) at which the observations were made. Simeon DeWitt, Geographer to the United States of America. [19]

By late summer of 1781 victory for the Continental Army was pretty well assured in the north, and Washington was laying plans for engaging the British forces in the southern colonies. Thus, from his New Brunswick, N. J., headquarters, the General on August 29, 1781, directed DeWitt that:

> Immediately upon receipt of this [letter] you will begin to Survey the road (if it has not been done already) to Princeton, thence (through Maidenhead) to Trenton, thence to Philadelphia, thence to the head of Elk through Darby, Chester, Wilmington [and] Christiana Bridge.
> At the head of Elk you will receive further orders. I need not observe to you the necessity of noting towns, Villages and remarkable Houses and places but I must desire that you will give me the rough traces of your Survey as you proceed on as I have reasons for desiring to know this as soon as possible. [20]

[18] Washington, *Writings*, ed. Fitzpatrick, XXI, 245–246, letter dated Feb. 19, 1781.
[19] *New York Packet and the American Advertiser*, August 30, 1781.
[20] Washington, *Writings*, ed. Fitzpatrick, XXIII, 68–69.

This job having apparently been completed, further instructions were sent on November 4, 1781, by Washington to DeWitt requesting that the latter:

. . . have the road from Williamsburgh by the way of Ruffens ferry, King William Court House, and Toddsbridge to the Bowling Green, or its unction with the Hanover Road Surveyed.
You will Survey the Road from Toddsbridge to Port Royal, thence to Hooes ferry, and from Hooes ferry on the Maryland side through Portobacco, Piscataway and the best and most direct road from thence to Baltimore.
The road from Bladensburg to Baltimore is also to be Surveyed, and a correct and connected map of the Roads from Kings ferry to York made out and delivered to me at Philadelphia on the North River.
You will receive Warrant on the Qr. Master General for the Sum of Twenty Pounds in Specie toward defraying your Expenses; And all Qr. Masters and Commissaries are hereby requested to furnish you with Provisions, forage and other Aids.[21]

This extensive mapping assignment was completed by DeWitt and his staff in time for the successful Yorktown Campaign. It is of interest to note that the southern routes shown in Colles' *Survey* correspond almost identically with those mentioned in Washington's directive to DeWitt. The road from "Hooes ferry on the Maryland side through Portobacco, Piscataway . . . and most direct road from thence to Baltimore" is not, however, in the *Survey*. It is possible that Colles may have intended to include these roads to complete his 100 plates, but the project terminated before this could be accomplished.

With the surrender of Cornwallis at Yorktown in October 1781, the ultimate victory of the Continental Army was assured. More than a year passed, however, before peace negotiations were completed. During this time DeWitt continued his services as Geographer-in-Chief, with headquarters in Philadelphia. There is no indication that further surveys were made, and he and his assistants were probably occupied in preparing composite and finished maps from rough survey drafts and in copying existing maps.

DeWitt had the vision to anticipate the need for good maps of the country, as well as for a cartographic summary of the war, and had plans to utilize the military surveys for preparing such maps. This idea he presented to headquarters in June 1783, with a request for

[21] *Ibid.*, XXIII, 332.

permission to utilize the official maps. Washington's aide, Jonathan Trumbull, replied on June 8, 1783, as follows:

> In consequence of your letter to me of the 4th instant, I have mentioned to the Comr. in Chief your purpose to obtain permission for publishing a Map of the State of War in America. His Excellency directs me to inform you, that the Measure is perfectly agreeable to him, and the proposition meets his full Approbation; it being his wish to see it accomplished in an accurate Manner, and at as early a period as the nature of the work will admit.[22]

Encouraged by Trumbull's letter, DeWitt wrote to the President of the Continental Congress on June 17, 1783, "praying leave and assistance to make and publish a complete map of the seat of the late war in America." [23] The committee to whom the request was referred reported "that though a map of the principal theatre of war in the middle states from actual surveys on a large scale is much desired such a work cannot in prudence be undertaken at the public expence in the present reduced state of our finances." [24]

There were some in the Congress who recognized the importance of preserving the documents and records of the war. Thus, on October 20, 1783, a resolution was passed "that the Geographers of the United States be instructed to deposit in the office of the Secretary of War a copy of whatever surveys have been made in their respective Departments." [25] We may assume that DeWitt complied with these instructions.

Later in 1783 DeWitt, anxious to get established in a civilian career requested a discharge from his duties as Geographer. On November 17 Washington acknowledged the request, but observed that "the nature of your Office being such as that Congress may possibly still have occasion for you, I cannot think myself at liberty to grant the Discharge you request; but circumstanced as you are I would advise that you make a final application to that Body, to know whether they are inclined to comply with your former application or whether they have any further occasion for your services." [26]

[22] *Ibid.*, XXVI, 496.
[23] Continental Congress, *Journal*, 1783, pp. 401–402.
[24] Continental Congress, *Journal*, 1783, p. 711.
[25] *Ibid.*
[26] Washington, *Writings*, ed. Fitzpatrick, XXVII, 244–245.

To make use of the military surveys was still very much on DeWitt's mind. A letter, sent to the President of the Continental Congress on January 12, 1784, offered another proposal for utilizing them:

> If the expense of bringing my maps to a further degree of perfection by additional survey, [he wrote,] be judged to be needless, I have this proposal to make. I will undertake, in the best manner I can from the materials I have, as much as shall be conveniently contained in one plate, and publish it at my own risque, provided I am furnished with cash sufficient for the purpose, on account of the pay now due me from the United States. . . . From the impressions of one plate I shall be able to judge, whether it shall afterwards answer to undertake any more at present.[27]

DeWitt dispatched a letter to Washington, who was now back at Mount Vernon, at the same time he submitted his proposal to the Continental Congress. The letter was delayed in transit, and Washington did not reply until March 3, 1784, when he wrote:

> I have urged, not only in public, but by private conversations with individual members of Congress, the policy, indeed the necessity of having accurate Maps of the United States, and they know full well my opinion of your worth, and ability to create them. All seem sensible to these, but the want of funds, I suppose, stops this, as it does so many other wheels which ought to move.
> The proposition contained in your Memr. of the 12th, to Congress, appear to me exceedingly reasonable and just: these sentiments I will express to a very valuable and much respected member of that Body to whom I am now writing.[28]

DeWitt's January 12 proposal was, on February 24, 1784, referred to a committee composed of Thomas Jefferson, Samuel Osgood, and Hugh Williamson. We might expect that these gentlemen gave it sympathetic consideration. There is, however, no record in the Journals of the Congress that a report was ever submitted on the request, and this DeWitt proposal also died for want of support.

Shortly after this disappointment, DeWitt resigned as Geographer-in-Chief, and on May 13, 1784, he was appointed Surveyor-General of New York State. This position he filled with distinction for more than fifty years and initiated and advanced many surveying and mapping projects within the state.

[27] T. Romeyn Beck, *Eulogium on Simeon DeWitt* (Albany, 1835), p. 10.
[28] Washington, *Writings*, ed. Fitzpatrick, XXVII, 347–348.

DeWitt took with him from the Geographer's Office drafts of a number of the military surveys that had been prepared under the direction of Robert Erskine and himself. In view of the Congressional directive previously noted that the military maps be deposited in the War Department, it is probable that those retained by DeWitt were in many instances the original field surveys. During the months following Yorktown, DeWitt's staff very likely prepared more finished copies of the maps for deposit in the War Department.

The Revolutionary War surveys were obviously highly valued by DeWitt and he hoped that he would some day be able to use them in publishing a map or maps of the war. This was not to be, however, and the manuscript maps remained for years, unutilized, in the possession of the DeWitt family. In 1845 they were presented, on behalf of DeWitt's son Richard Varick DeWitt, to the New-York Historical Society.[29]

It would be convenient to assume that DeWitt in 1788 or 1789 loaned his original manuscript maps to Colles to be used in compiling the latter's *Survey of the Roads of the United States.* Unfortunately there is in the record of neither of the two men a suggestion of any personal relations or contacts, although very likely they were acquainted with each other's work. Colles obviously was informed about the military surveys and of DeWitt's contribution to their preparation. A possible contact between the two men might have been established through General George Clinton, Governor of New York State, who was Simeon DeWitt's uncle and a close friend of Colles' associate and benefactor, Gen. John Lamb. There is no positive evidence that such a contact was established, however, and we cannot assume that this was the channel through which Colles gained access to the Erskine-DeWitt maps.

It is more likely that in this instance, as he did on frequent other similar occasions during his lifetime, Colles sought aid from close friends and associates. During the Revolution and in the post-war years, one of his principal benefactors was John Lamb. The latter's superior, during much of the war, was General Henry Knox. As we have seen (in his letter to Washington in 1783) Colles, too, had apparently worked with Knox and offered the latter's name as a reference

[29] *New-York Historical Society: Proceedings* (1845), p. 21.

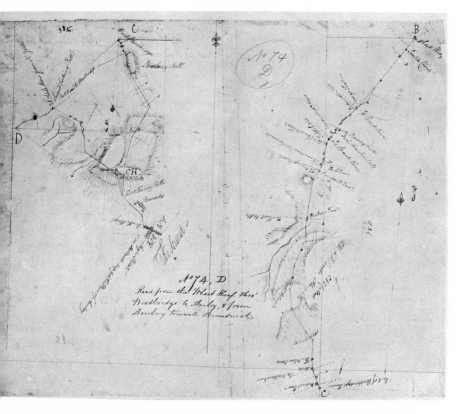

Fig. 20. Many of the Erskine-DeWitt maps are rough, manuscript, field sketches, such as this one which shows a part of New Jersey. This reproduction and Figures 18 and 19 have been greatly reduced in size. Courtesy of the New-York Historical Society, New York City.

to Washington. General Knox remained with the army until January 1784, when he returned to his home in Dorchester, Massachusetts. He was not to remain there long, however, for in March 1785 he accepted from the Continental Congress appointment as Secretary of War. After the Constitution was ratified and the first President inaugurated in 1789, Knox was reappointed to this office in Washington's cabinet.

Among the responsibilities of the War Department was the custody and preservation of the records of the war. These undoubtedly included maps and surveys, which, under the Congressional resolution of October 20, 1783, the Geographers of the United States were "instructed to deposit in the office of the Secretary of War." DeWitt did not resign as Geographer-in-Chief until six months later, and we can expect that he complied with the resolution. Support for this assumption is found in

71

the fact that many of the maps retained by DeWitt and now preserved in the New-York Historical Society, are rough field surveys (Fig. 20). In the several years between the British defeat at Yorktown and his departure from the army, DeWitt and his staff had ample time to prepare copies for deposit in the War Department.

A set of the military surveys was, we may therefore expect, in the custody of General Knox's War Department in 1788 or 1789, when Christopher Colles was desperately trying to complete his *Survey of the Roads*. There can be little doubt that the mentally alert and resourceful Colles was aware of the existence and location of the maps. He probably looked to his friend, Gen. Lamb, for help in obtaining them. As one of Knox's most reliable artillery officers, Lamb undoubtedly had access to his former commander. Knox apparently saw no objection to making the maps available to Colles, who, as we have seen, had also contributed to the success of Knox's Artillery Department during the Revolution.

This assumption unfortunately can be neither verified nor disproved. Many of the early War Department records were destroyed by fire in 1800. Those currently extant in the U. S. National Archives do not include any military maps nor any record of their transfer to or use by Colles. It seems more plausible, however, that he acquired the maps from the War Department than from DeWitt. Just how he secured the military surveys, however, remains an unanswered question, open to conjecture and debate.

# VIII

# The Erskine-DeWitt Maps and Colles' *Survey*

In information presented, Colles' *Survey* and the Erskine-DeWitt military maps have much in common. In format and cartographic representation they are, however, quite dissimilar. The latter are of two types. Most numerous are rough manuscript drafts, probably made in the field, of various roads. They are oriented, in the conventional manner, with north at the top of the sheet. The maps have no marginal lines, and many of the names are in cursive.

Some Erskine-DeWitt maps are more finished compilations, or "contractions" as they are called, and contain information derived from a number of field sketches. The "contractions" are smaller in scale, cover a considerable section of country, and have titles and borders. Names are, for the most part, neatly lettered on the maps.

The maps in Colles' road book are of the "strip" type, with two or three sections on each plate. The area portrayed is limited to the roads and the country immediately bordering them, and the strips are arranged on the plates and within the book in continuous sequence. There is no attempt to orient the maps with the pages, and arrows are used to indicate compass north. Each plate has a single line border, and is identified with a number and a descriptive title. Names are neatly lettered on the maps.

The strip map format was commonly used in road books of the eighteenth century, and Colles undoubtedly patterned his *Survey* after them. This format was introduced by John Ogilby about 1675, and was continued in subsequent British and Irish books for more than a hundred years (Fig. 21).

The origin of this form even antedates Ogilby, however, and the strip map was used for earlier French road books and for some of the itineraries that guided devout pilgrims to and from the Holy Land

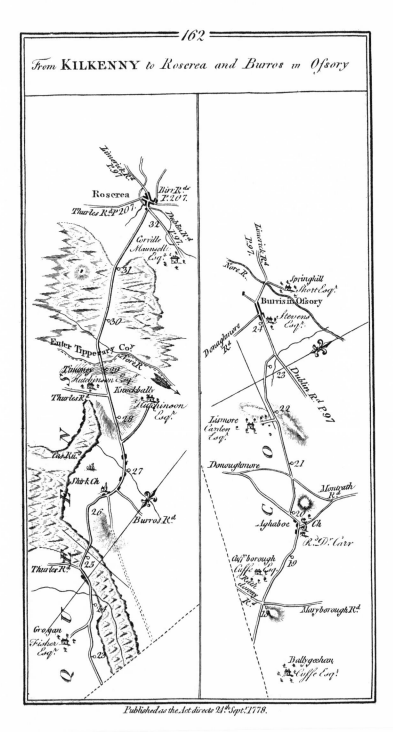

Fig. 21. The format used by Colles in his *Survey* was patterned after that common in British and Irish road books of the eighteenth century. This plate, from Taylor and Skinner's *Maps of the Roads of Ireland*, London & Dublin, 1778, shows the region where Colles lived prior to his emigration to America. Note the similarity in format to plates in the *Survey*. Courtesy of the Library of Congress.

during the Crusades. The Peutinger Table, one of the few extant examples of Roman cartography, is also in the form of a strip map.

Besides following a long-established precedent for road books, Colles' strip map format was adapted to the geographic conditions of the period. Away from the coast and the major streams, roads were the only avenues of communication. Settlements and farmsteads were strung along these arteries like beads on a string. Cleared lands, in many parts of the country, extended only a few hundred yards from the road, and in some areas the highway was only a narrow lane hacked through the forest. Strip maps of the roads included, therefore, most of the settled regions and provided all the information needed by a traveler.

In symbolism, as in format, the maps in Colles' *Survey* differ from the Erskine-DeWitt military maps. The former, in general, have more and varied symbols while the latter use word descriptions for some features. On the title page of Colles' road book there is a legend, or list of "References," with eight symbols and the names of the features they represent. Additional conventional signs, not here listed, are found on certain of the plates.

Among the physical features shown on Colles' maps are rivers and streams, lakes, trees, marshes or swamps, and hills. The latter are portrayed by crude hachures or series of short parallel lines. The hill and tree symbols are used less freely on the early plates than on later ones.

Double lines represent roads on Colles' maps, whereas they are shown by single lines on the military field sketches. On the Erskine-DeWitt composite maps, or "contractions," roads are often indicated by dotted lines. Ferries are located and frequently named by Colles, and bridges are shown by continuing the road symbol, unbroken, across the river or stream. At cross roads and intersections arrows point to the towns or villages to which they lead.

Cultural features are quite numerous on the *Survey* maps. They provide a cross section of the interests and activities of the period. Towns and villages are portrayed by solid squares or rectangles strung along both sides of the road or clustered at intersections. Individual farmsteads are also shown with solid squares or rectangles, and the name of the occupant is given.

75

Taverns (or ordinaries, as they were still called in the south) were essential alike to travelers and to permanent residents, and they are clearly marked on both map series. The symbol used by Colles was probably intended to represent the familiar post that stood, with its distinctive sign, before most inns. It also suggests, however, a gallows or gibbet. Names of tavern owners or proprietors are lettered beside the symbol. An open rectangle (also used for farmsteads) with the name, identifies taverns on the military surveys.

A flared circle, probably meant to symbolize a water wheel, locates grist mills in Colles' road book. The same symbol is used for other mills (for example, saw mills, fulling mills), but these are also identified by function. A similar symbol locates iron works on Erskine-DeWitt maps. Quite a few are shown, probably because of Erskine's personal interest in iron manufacturing.

Blacksmith shops, the service stations of this day, are marked on Colles' maps by a representation of a horseshoe. Courthouses, town houses, meeting houses, and "gaols" (jails) are among the public buildings identified in the *Survey*.

Two types of churches are separately symbolized, Episcopal by crosses, and Presbyterian by an X over a vertical line ($\frac{x}{1}$). Churches of other denominations are indicated by the appropriate name. On the Erskine-DeWitt maps houses of worship are shown by a pictorial representation of a church. Colles marks burying grounds with an orderly pattern of short parallel lines, obviously meant to suggest graves.

Information shown on the *Survey* maps is unusually detailed and complete. We must agree with Colles that:

A traveller will here find so plain and circumstantial a description of the road, that whilst he has the draft with him it will be impossible for him to miss his way: he will have the satisfaction of knowing the names of many of the persons who reside on the road; if his horse should want a shoe, or his carriage be broke, he will by the bare inspection of the draft be able to determine whether he must go backward or forward to a blacksmith's shop. Persons who have houses or plantations on the road may in case they want to let, lease, or sell the same, advertise in the public newspapers that the place is marked in such a page of Colles' Survey of the roads; this will give so particular a description of its situation that no difficulty or doubt will

emain about it. . . . It is expected many other entertaining and useful
urposes will be discovered when these surveys come into general use.[1]

Undoubtedly Colles' *Survey of the Roads* was, as one historical
writer has stated, "one of the most generally useful books of the post-
revolutionary period in the United States.[2] If we accept this appraisal,
we may wonder why the road book apparently was so unprofitable to
its publisher that it was abandoned before all the intended plates were
issued. Some of the prominent persons of the time, including Washington and Jefferson, had copies of the *Survey* in their libraries. The road
book, however, seems not to have been purchased in any great numbers by travelers, the market to which it was specifically directed.

There was considerable travel in the United States following the
Revolutionary War, both by Americans and by visitors from Europe.
However, inasmuch as transportation was for most persons by public
stage along a few well-established roads, individual travelers relied
upon the coach drivers to get them to their destination. Apparently
few of them personally felt the need for a map of the roads. It may be
that Colles was once again ahead of his time, and the public was not
yet ready for such a guide.

Other factors contributing to the failure of the road book probably
included the absence of maps of all but a small section of New England, one of the most populous and traveled regions, ineffective and
inadequate distribution outlets (the *Survey* seems to have been available only in New York and Philadelphia), serial publication (which
particularly limited its usefulness to foreign travelers), and the probable small number printed. Operating as Colles was, with little or no
capital, it is doubtful whether the editions of the different map series
numbered more than several hundred copies.

Failure of the road book seems not to have discouraged Colles'
cartographic interest. Several years after work on the *Survey* terminated, he launched an even more ambitious map publishing venture.
In 1794 there was issued, over the imprint of John Buel of New York,

[1] Colles, *Proposals for Publishing*.
[2] Edmund C. Morgan, "The Colonial Scene 1602–1800, An Annotated List of
Books, Broadsides, Prints and Maps . . . Based on an Exhibit at John Carter
Brown Library in May, 1949," in *American Antiquarian Society: Proceedings*,
vol. 60 (April 19, 1950–Oct. 18, 1950), p. 141.

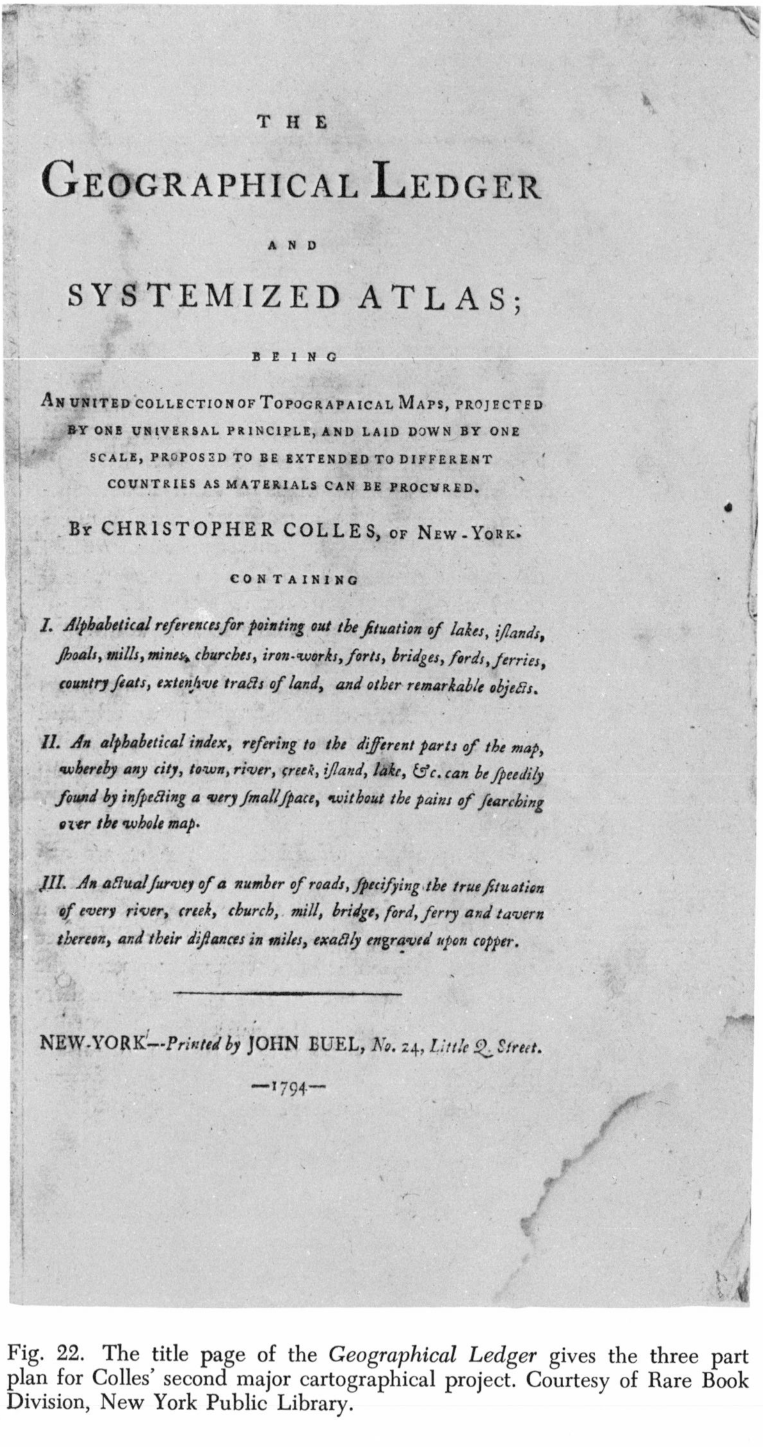

THE

# GEOGRAPHICAL LEDGER

A N D

# SYSTEMIZED ATLAS;

B E I N G

AN UNITED COLLECTION OF TOPOGRAPAICAL MAPS, PROJECTED
BY ONE UNIVERSAL PRINCIPLE, AND LAID DOWN BY ONE
SCALE, PROPOSED TO BE EXTENDED TO DIFFERENT
COUNTRIES AS MATERIALS CAN BE PROCURED.

By CHRISTOPHER COLLES, of New-York.

CONTAINING

I. *Alphabetical references for pointing out the situation of lakes, islands,
shoals, mills, mines, churches, iron-works, forts, bridges, fords, ferries,
country seats, extensive tracts of land, and other remarkable objects.*

II. *An alphabetical index, refering to the different parts of the map,
whereby any city, town, river, creek, island, lake, &c. can be speedily
found by inspecting a very small space, without the pains of searching
over the whole map.*

III. *An actual survey of a number of roads, specifying the true situation
of every river, creek, church, mill, bridge, ford, ferry and tavern
thereon, and their distances in miles, exactly engraved upon copper.*

NEW-YORK---*Printed by* JOHN BUEL, *No.* 24, *Little Q. Street.*

—1794—

Fig. 22. The title page of the *Geographical Ledger* gives the three part
plan for Colles' second major cartographical project. Courtesy of Rare Book
Division, New York Public Library.

prospectus and several plates for a *Geographical Ledger and Systematized Atlas*, by Christopher Colles. The work was registered for copyright at New York on June 7, 1794 (Fig. 22).

The *Ledger* was planned as a loose-leaf atlas, with each plate constituting a section of a large map of the country laid down on a common projection. The scale is ten miles to an inch, and each plate extends over two degrees of latitude and four degrees of longitude.

Sheets are numbered according to a common plan and include, as well, numbers of adjoining plates. Physical and cultural features are identified on the maps by a series of code letters keyed to an index. Because of this indexing system Colles wrote in the prospectus that "I have given this work the name of the Geographical Ledger, as the situation of places can be found (by means of the index and references) as speedily as a merchant can find any particular account in his ledger."

Colles' *Geographical Ledger* was apparently even less successful than his *Survey*, and only five plates of the former are known. When joined they form a map covering most of New England, New York, and parts of Pennsylvania and New Jersey.

Colles' plan for the *Ledger* called for three parts. The first was an alphabetical reference "for pointing out the situation of lakes, islands . . country seats, extensive tracts of land, and other remarkable objects." This was followed by "an alphabetical index refering to the different parts of the map whereby any city, town, river, creek, island, lake &c. can be speedily found." The third portion of the *Ledger* was to be "an actual survey of a number of roads, specifying the true situation of every river, creek, church, mill, bridge, ford, ferry and tavern thereon, and their distances in miles, exactly engraved upon copper." This indicates that Colles planned to incorporate into the *Geographical Ledger* the plates originally prepared for his *Survey of the Roads.*

The five known plates, and the title page, prospectus, and several pages of index, now preserved in a few libraries, are probably the only parts of the *Ledger* that were issued. As Griffin has suggested, "Colles' chronic poverty [probably] precluded his supplying the capital necessary to continue the series." [3] Another reason for the failure of Colles'

[3] Griffin, "Colles and His Two American Map Series," p. 181.

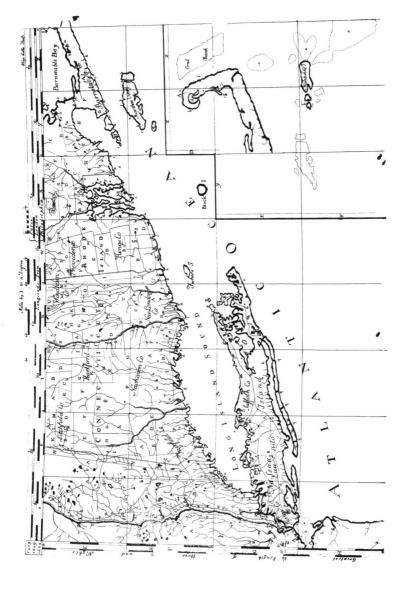

Fig. 23. This map, considerably reduced from the original, is one of five plates prepared for the *Geographical Ledger*. Note the engraving credit, "Eliza Colles Sculp.," in the upper right corner. The letters on the face of the map were part of the ingenious indexing system devised by Colles and were keyed to an alphabetical list of names. Courtesy of the Library of Congress.

artographic ventures undoubtedly was that "he was attempting to orce a thoughtful and systematic plan for mapping a new nation on a public which was unwilling — and perhaps unable — to sustain it." [4]

It is interesting to note that two of the plates in the Ledger (nos. 1549 & 1569) carry a credit to "Eliza Colles, Sculp.," who was apparently one of Colles' daughters (Fig. 23). There appears to be no other record of engravings prepared by her, although, as noted above, Benson J. Lossing in his *History of New York City* (1884) states that the maps in the *Survey* were engraved by Colles' daughter.[5]

Little is known about Colles' family. Before leaving Ireland, his wife had borne him six children, of whom four were living when the family sailed for America. An infant child died during the voyage and was buried at sea.

Colles is said to have fathered eleven children. It is probable that he married twice, for in reporting Colles' death John Pintard wrote, "I shall strictly perform to see his remains deposit[d] along side those of his first wife." [6]

Most of the children apparently did not attain adulthood. The Census of 1790 records the Colles household as comprising one male head of family, one male under 16 years of age, and four females. The New York City Directory for 1791 lists "Richard and John Colles, Paper Stainers." The latter was Christopher's cousin, previously mentioned, and "Richard was apparently the eldest son of . . . Christopher." [7] Eliza was undoubtedly one of the three Colles daughters listed in the 1790 census.

Colles' children either preceded him in death or established homes of their own elsewhere than in New York City. At any rate, when the toil-worn engineer was laid in his grave, none of his family were present at the funeral service. Moreover, descendants bearing the Colles name today trace their lineage in America back to cousin John rather than to Christopher.

[4] *Ibid.*, p. 182.
[5] Lossing, *History of New York City*, p. 75.
[6] John Pintard, *Letters to His Daughter Eliza N. P. Davidson* (New York, 1940), letter dated Oct. 3, 1816, p. 29.
[7] DeForest, *James Colles*, pp. 6–7.

# IX

# Latter Years

Following abandonment of the road book project and prior to launching *The Geographical Ledger*, Christopher Colles had another brief affair with his first love, canals. In fact the opportunity to work on the canal project may have been a factor in bringing the *Survey* project to an abrupt end.

Internal improvements were very much in the minds of Americans in the early years of the Republic. While water transport was still the most economical means of moving goods, there were natural barriers and obstructions along many streams which limited their utilization. This was true for the Connecticut River, whose several falls and rapids interrupted transport. It was inevitable that sooner or later attempts would be made to eliminate the natural obstructions.

Public funds, as we have seen, were not available for internal improvements at this early date. Fortunately, European capitalists saw in the new nation an opportunity for favorable investments. Thus, early in 1792 a group of Dutch bankers, associated with several local promoters and engineers, was granted a charter to improve navigation on the Connecticut River.

Constructing canals at South Hadley Falls and Turners Falls were among the company's early projects. The directors engaged Christopher Colles to prepare surveys at both sites. Records indicate that he commenced work at South Hadley on May 21, 1792, and at Turners Falls on July 3 of the same year.[1]

How Colles came to be selected for the Connecticut River surveys we do not know. Qualified engineers, however, were a rarity at the time, and his reputation in this field no doubt extended beyond the

[1] Timothy Dwight, *Travels in New England and New York* (New Haven, 1821), I, 322, and Lyman S. Hayes, "The navigation of the Connecticut River," in *Vermont Historical Society: Proceedings, 1915–1916*, p. 75.

imits of New York City. This seems to have been one of the few occasions, during his career in America, when Colles was employed as an
engineer. Most of the engineering projects in which he was involved
were personally sponsored.

Construction on the South Hadley Canal began on April 20, 1793,
and work was completed in the fall of 1794. The canal, two and a third
miles long and largely cut through solid rock, was opened to traffic in
the spring of 1795. Boats were raised from one level to another by
means of an inclined plane. This system proved to be not wholly
satisfactory, however, and was later replaced by locks. The South
Hadley Canal was one of the earliest completed in the United States.

Actual construction of the canal was directed by Benjamin Prescott
of Northampton, Massachusetts. Colles' contribution was apparently
limited to making the initial surveys, which, as noted above, were
completed during the summer of 1792. That fall he probably returned
to New York City and shortly after began work on the *Geographical
Ledger*.

This project was short-lived, and its demise probably occurred no
later than 1795. Considering the rarity of extant copies, the *Ledger*
was probably a more drastic failure than the *Survey of the Roads*.
Griffin suggests that Colles' "affairs may very possibly have been in
such a critical state that he found it impossible to continue the serial
publication of *The Geographical Ledger*.[2] Moreover, he observes that
John Buel, the publisher of the *Ledger*, like Colles was not very
successful and was forced to abandon other enterprises.

The next decade was unusually hard on Christopher Colles. We can
only conjecture as to how he eked out an existence, for data on these
years is almost wholly lacking. We have noted previously that in 1797
Colles' name appeared on a list of applicants desirous of providing a
water system for New York City. The application, which was not
successful, was Colles' final attempt to help solve the city's water
supply problem.

Did the failure of his cartographic projects force the unfortunate
engineer to leave New York once again? It is possible that his financial
setbacks may even have landed him for a time in prison. Prior to the
passage of the Federal bankruptcy acts about 1800, the law was ex-

[2] Griffin, "Colles and His Two American Map Series," p. 182.

ceedingly harsh on debtors. Even so stalwart a citizen as John Pintard was interned for several years because of an unfortunate financial transaction.

Dr. John Francis, Colles' friend and biographer, lends support to the possibility that he was away from New York for at least part of these uncertain years. He recalled that his versatile friend had, among other occupations, engaged in "practical land-surveying and taught it in different parts of [New York] State and elsewhere." [3] More positive evidence that Colles was out of the city for part of this time is found in the 1808 pamphlet, previously cited, which advanced the idea for a timber canal across northern New Jersey. Data in the pamphlet and for the detailed map which accompanied it undoubtedly were based on personal surveys. Just when they were carried out we do not know, but it was probably after 1800.

During this period, too, Colles suffered the loss of one of his dearest friends and benefactors, Gen. John Lamb. Following resignation from the Artillery, Lamb was in 1784 appointed Collector of Customs of the Port of New York by the State Legislature. Notwithstanding Lamb's strong anti-Federalist activities, when the Constitution was ratified, President Washington in August 1789 placed the veteran soldier in charge of the Federal Customs Office in New York.

A large shortage was discovered in the Customs Office accounts in 1797. Although the discrepancy was traced to a former employee, Lamb as Director was held responsible. To recompense the loss, he sold his lands and property and resigned the directorship. Three years later the Revolutionary hero and onetime leader of the Sons of Liberty in New York City died in discredit and poverty. Lamb's misfortune and death no doubt profoundly affected Colles and may have contributed to his decision to leave New York.

Colles' pamphlet describing the timber canal was published in New York in 1808, and suggests that he had by this time returned to the city. There is no record of any enterprise with which he was associated for the next several years.

During these undocumented years we may assume that the engineer-philosopher earned a few coppers from his public lectures and exhibits. Francis believed that "perhaps the luckiest of his scientific hits was

[3] Francis, "Reminiscences of Colles," p. 198.

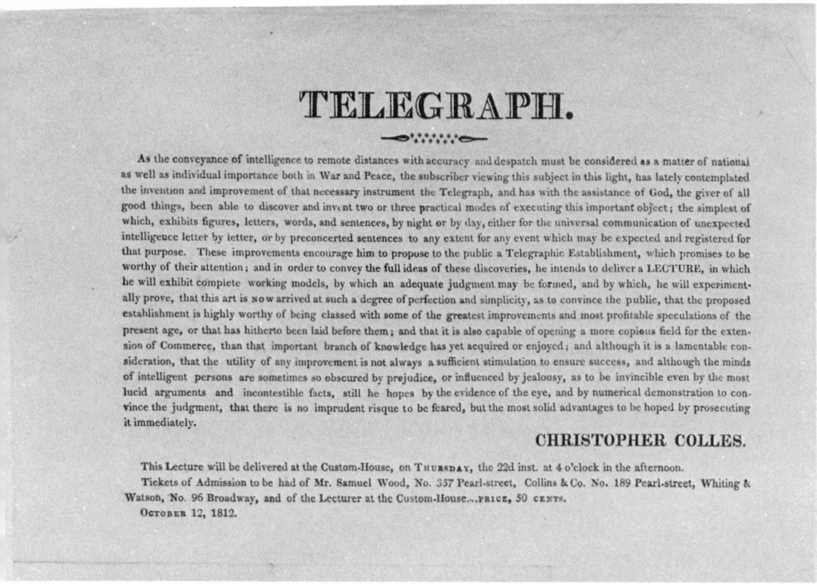

# TELEGRAPH.

As the conveyance of intelligence to remote distances with accuracy and despatch must be considered as a matter of national as well as individual importance both in War and Peace, the subscriber viewing this subject in this light, has lately contemplated the invention and improvement of that necessary instrument the Telegraph, and has with the assistance of God, the giver of all good things, been able to discover and invent two or three practical modes of executing this important object; the simplest of which, exhibits figures, letters, words, and sentences, by night or by day, either for the universal communication of unexpected intelligence letter by letter, or by preconcerted sentences to any extent for any event which may be expected and registered for that purpose. These improvements encourage him to propose to the public a Telegraphic Establishment, which promises to be worthy of their attention; and in order to convey the full ideas of these discoveries, he intends to deliver a LECTURE, in which he will exhibit complete working models, by which an adequate judgment may be formed, and by which, he will experimentally prove, that this art is now arrived at such a degree of perfection and simplicity, as to convince the public, that the proposed establishment is highly worthy of being classed with some of the greatest improvements and most profitable speculations of the present age, or that has hitherto been laid before them; and that it is also capable of opening a more copious field for the extension of Commerce, than that important branch of knowledge has yet acquired or enjoyed; and although it is a lamentable consideration, that the utility of any improvement is not always a sufficient stimulation to ensure success, and although the minds of intelligent persons are sometimes so obscured by prejudice, or influenced by jealousy, as to be invincible even by the most lucid arguments and incontestible facts, still he hopes by the evidence of the eye, and by numerical demonstration to convince the judgment, that there is no imprudent risque to be feared, but the most solid advantages to be hoped by prosecuting it immediately.

**CHRISTOPHER COLLES.**

This Lecture will be delivered at the Custom-House, on THURSDAY, the 22d inst. at 4 o'clock in the afternoon.

Tickets of Admission to be had of Mr. Samuel Wood, No. 357 Pearl-street, Collins & Co. No. 189 Pearl-street, Whiting & Watson, No. 96 Broadway, and of the Lecturer at the Custom-House...PRICE, 50 CENTS.

OCTOBER 12, 1812.

Fig. 24. Colles emphasized the importance of a fast medium for long distance communication in this broadside announcing a lecture on his semaphoric telegraph system. Courtesy of the New-York Historical Society, New York City.

the application he made of his telescope and microscope. The casual pittance of a six-penny piece for a look at Venus, or the circulation, through the web of a frog's foot . . . proved adequate to his fullest desires." [4] One writer visualizes Colles "standing in City Hall Park with his telescope set up, asking the passer-by if he would like to see Jupiter for sixpence, 'or, if you have no sixpence, I will let you see it for nothing.'" [5]

It was 1812, and Christopher Colles was in his seventy-fourth year. His frail body was worn and bent, but his mind was still agile and projecting big ideas. The last of his ingenious inventions was the semaphoric telegraph, which he presented for public consideration in 1812. A broadside published in that year announced that Christopher Colles had "invented two or three practical modes of executing the conveyance of intelligence to remote areas with accuracy and dispatch" [6] (Fig. 24). The several devices were described in a lecture presented on October 22.

[4] Ibid., p. 200.
[5] DeForest, James Colles, p. 10.
[6] Christopher Colles, telegraph broadside.

85

# DESCRIPTION

## OF THE NUMERICAL

# TELEGRAPH.

For communicating unexpected intelligence
by figures, letters, words, and sentences,
with directions for writing the correspondence either public or private, and shewing
the manner of working the machine with
perfect accuracy and despatch.

## BY CHRISTOPHER COLLES,

### OF NEW-YORK.

*BROOKLYN:*

PRINTED BY ALDEN SPOONER.

1813.

Fig. 25. Title page of booklet in which Christopher Colles described his numerical telegraph and showed "the manner of working the machine with perfect accuracy and despatch." Courtesy of Peabody Institute Library, Baltimore, Maryland.

The principle of the semaphoric telegraph was outlined by Colles in a pamphlet published in 1813 (Fig. 25). The device, which was capable of transmitting 84 letters in five minutes, was apparently an adaption of and improvement on one that had been earlier developed in France. Colles' telegraph was described as a system "which exhibits figures, letters, words and sentences . . . either for the universal communication of unexpected intelligence letter by letter, or by preconcerted sentences to any extent, for any event which may be expected and registered for that purpose." [7] The machine "composed of a frame of timber in the form of a five-pointed star, [was] to be erected on eminences, so as to be distinctly visible with a telescope at a distance of ten miles. A revolving index carried a circular board, on which were marked the nine digits and a cypher" [8] (Fig. 26).

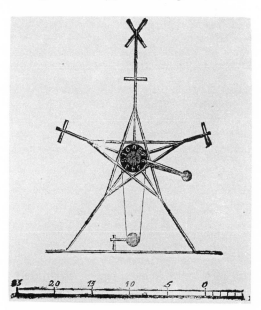

Fig. 26. The numerical telegraph here illustrated was the last of many Colles inventions. Courtesy of Peabody Institute Library, Baltimore, Maryland.

[7] Henry O'Rielly, "Material for Telegraph History," *The Historical Magazine*, V (April, 1869), 262.

[8] J. A. Stevens, "Christopher Colles," *Magazine of American History*, II (1878), 346–347.

The aging, though still visionary, Colles pictured a semaphoric telegraphic network extending from Maine to New Orleans along the entire Atlantic and Gulf coasts. Despite the need, demonstrated during the War of 1812, for some form of rapid communication, Colles' telegraph was only placed in service between New York City and Sandy Hook, New Jersey. Some accounts state that the versatile old inventor operated the system during the War of 1812. There seems to be some doubt, however, whether the telegraph was constructed before 1816.

The Minutes of the New York City Common Council, for August 12, 1816, note that:

. . . the Committee on the subject of Telegraphic communication Reported that it was understood the object of this establishment was to accomodate the Ship Owners and other Merchants of our City, who propose to provide for the expence thereof and wished the Corporation, being a public body and the general representative of the City to direct the execution agency of the undertaking.[9]

The report further indicated that:

. . . the proposed communication would require three Telegraphs one at Sandy Hook, one upon the Highlands of Staten Island, and one at the Battery, that the buildings & machinery which must be necessarily erected would not cost less than two thousand Dollars & that two men for each telegraph must be employed at an expense of about Two thousand Dollars per annum.[10]

The report of the City Council further noted that New York merchants:

. . . expressed much zeal for the accomplishment of [the telegraph project], and have put into the hands of your Committee, an agreement subscribed by about one hundred and fifty of their constituents proposing that each Vessel arriving at this Port, by way of Sandy Hook from a foreign Country, should pay one Dollar and every Coasting Vessel arriving through the same Channel should pay half a Dollar.[11]

Notwithstanding the profferred support of the Merchants, the Council Committee recommended that "it is inexpedient for the Corporation to take any further measures in this business" because of the anticipated

[9] Quoted in Edward H. Hall, "Early Pipe Line Projects," p. 688.
[10] Ibid., p. 689.
[11] Ibid.

difficulty of collecting fees from incoming ships.[12] It further proposed that "as [Christopher Colles] has . . . been employed by your Committee . . . that One hundred and fifty Dollars be paid for his services."[13]

Whether or not the merchants were able to finance the telegraph without the help of the city we do not know. Several authorities affirm, however, that Colles succeeded in "getting his Telegraph constructed so far as to signalize intelligence between New York City and Sandy Hook . . . which short section he managed for several years."[14]

The semaphoric telegraph, at any rate, was short-lived, and like so many of Colles' ideas and inventions brought him little personal gain. Historians, however, credit the resourceful engineer with having been the first publicly to introduce to the country a practical system of telecommunication. "The mode of correspondence by numerals, referring to words and sentences, as proposed by Colles in 1812," O'Rielly notes, "was substantially like that temporarily adopted twenty or more years later by Prof. Morse."[15]

While awaiting favorable action by the City Council on his telegraph, Colles relied again upon lectures and exhibits for a meager income. The *Columbian Magazine* for July 1816 carried a notice of an exhibition by him of "a number of new mechanical contrivances of his own invention."[16]

About this time the City of New York completed a new building to shelter its poor and indigent citizens. Accordingly,

. . . a number of learned societies, afterwards grouped under the general name of the New York Institution, applied to the Common Council for the use of the old almshouse as their headquarters; and on May 13, 1816 the Common Council directed that leases for occupying the almshouse be executed to the New York Society Library and Philosophical Society of New York, the New York Historical Society, the New York Academy of Fine Arts, John Griscomb, Professor of Chemistry; John Scudder, proprietor of the American Museum; and "certain gentlemen as trustees of the U. S. Military and Philosophical Society."[17]

[12] *Ibid.*
[13] *Ibid.*, pp. 689–690.
[14] O'Rielly, "Material for Telegraph History," p. 263.
[15] *Ibid.*, p. 263.
[16] *Columbian Magazine* (New York), July 1816.
[17] Hall, "Early Pipe Line Projects," pp. 690–691.

Through the influence of his good friend, John Pintard, Christopher Colles was "appointed to take charge of the old Alms House Buildings lately assigned to the use of certain literary establishments." [18]

But time was running out for the aged engineer and philosopher, and he enjoyed for only a brief period the security and shelter afforded by the appointment as curator and custodian of the New York Institution building. It was here that Christopher Colles' long and toilsome life ended. John Pintard writes of his last days in letters to his daughter Eliza N. Pintard Davidson. On October 3, 1816, he reported:

> I have just returned from the New York Institution in which I had placed a little old man Mr. Colles, who was to have acted as door keeper of the Academy. He is fast travelling to a better world, was taken with an ague & fever last week. Of a slender attenuated frame, in his 79th year, his stamina are quite worn out & he is falling gently into the arms of his Redeemer, for a purer more innocent being never existed. I have long been his only friend, I mean active friend, for he never wanted for kind words, & always promised what I shall strictly perform to see his remains deposit[d] along side those of his first wife in St. Pauls Church Yard. His lamp is nearly extinguished, nor shall I probably hear his voice again.[19]

The following day Pintard noted that, "My old friend still exists. I went to see [him] just after six [A.M.]. The *Vis Vitae* is very powerful in him & he may last a day or two." [20] The end, however, came that night. "My old friend & philosopher," Pintard wrote on Saturday, October 5, "expired last evening half past 11, without much struggle. I thought he knew my voice when I spoke to him for the last time yes[y] morning. Tomorrow at 5 p.m. I shall render him the last services. Requiescat in pace." [21]

On Sunday, October 6, 1816, the mortal remains of Christopher Colles were laid to rest in the yard of St. Paul's Episcopal Church (Fig. 27). The only mourners, besides the officiating cleric, were his faithful companions and benefactors, John Pintard and Dr. John W. Francis. As previously noted, no stone marks the grave, and its precise location in the cemetery is unknown.

There are conflicting records concerning Colles' age at the time of

[18] New York City Common Council, Minutes of July 22, 1816.
[19] Pintard, *Letters to His Daughter*, I, letter dated Oct. 3, 1816, p. 29.
[20] *Ibid.*, letter dated Oct. 4, 1816, p. 30.
[21] *Ibid.*, letter dated Oct. 5, 1816, p. 30.

T. Anderson del.                                          Scoles, sculp.

*A View of St. Paul's Church, New-York.*

Fig. 27. As reported by John Pintard, the body of Christopher Colles was laid to rest in St. Paul's Church Yard on October 6, 1816. From *New York Magazine*, October 1795. Courtesy of the Library of Congress.

his death. Pintard states he was in his seventy-ninth year (i.e., 78 years old) when he died. In a memorial to Colles, published some years later, Dr. Francis erroneously states that "his death took place in the fall of 1821, at the advanced age of eighty-four years." [22] According to the best evidence, Christopher Colles was born May 9, 1739. On October 4, 1816, when he died, he had, therefore, attained the age of 77 years, four months and 28 days.

As described by Dr. Francis, Colles in his later years was a "little weather-beaten old man, small in stature, and attenuated in frame, of weight some one hundred and ten points avoirdupois." [23] Francis noted, too, that "there was something very engaging in the physiognomy of Colles. He was naturally cheerful and buoyant, at times pensive, yet free from any corrosive melancholy. His ample front, his sparse white locks, his cavernous gray eyes, with that weakness which often marks old age, betokened a resigned spirit." [24]

The features of Christopher Colles have been preserved for posterity by his friend, John Wesley Jarvis, the noted portraitist (Frontispiece). "My pencil," said Jarvis to Colles, "will render you hereafter better known. You have done too much good to be forgotten." [25] The Jarvis portrait is in the collections of the New-York Historical Society and was probably personally presented to that institution by the artist.[26] Another portrait, picturing a somewhat younger Colles, by James Frothingham, is owned by the Metropolitan Museum of Art. It was presented to that institution in 1917 by the pioneer engineer's namesake, Dr. Christopher John Colles (Fig. 28).

Colles' industry and energy were widely recognized. Throughout "a long life [he] knew no idle hour . . . his conversation was instructive and his genius in mechanics sufficiently original to command approbation. His nature was benevolent: his morals void of offence toward God and man." [27]

Christopher Colles had a lovable and engaging personality. Not-

[22] Francis, "Reminiscences of Colles," p. 207.
[23] *Ibid.*, p. 197.
[24] *Ibid.*, p. 208.
[25] *Ibid.*, p. 201.
[26] Harold E. Dickson, *John Wesley Jarvis, American Painter, 1780–1840* (New York, 1949), p. ix.
[27] Francis, "Reminiscences of Colles," p. 201.

Fig. 28. This portrait of Colles by James Frothingham was presented to the Metropolitan Museum by a member of the Colles family. Courtesy of The Metropolitan Museum of Art, Gift of Dr. Christopher J. Colles, 1917.

withstanding his modest and unassuming character, "everybody seemed to know [him]; no one spoke disparagingly of him. His enthusiasm, his restlessness were familiar to the citizens at large. He, in short, was a part of our domestic history." [28] Newspaper reports of Colles' death affirmed that "he was as honest a man as ever lived, and notwithstanding his mechanical eccentricities, was respected by all who knew him." [29]

Measured by practical and material standards, the career of Chris-

[28] *Ibid.*, p. 202.
[29] *New York Gazette and General Advertiser*, October 7, 1816.

topher Colles was one of almost complete failure. None of the ambi
tious projects and ideas he conceived and initiated was carried throug|
to successful accomplishment. His pathway through life was littered
with shattered dreams and unrealized hopes. The times when he and
his family had even the basic necessities of life were infrequent.

For one who enjoyed so little success in life, it is somewhat surpris
ing to note the many laudatory words spoken and written about him
after death. He was, wrote O'Rielly, "one of the remarkable persons o
his time, and was so recognized by such men as DeWitt Clinton, Cad
wallader D. Colden, Charles King, Dr. Hosack, Dr. J. W. Francis
and other prominent gentlemen acquainted with his valuable and
unobtrusive career." [30] Colden, in his *Memoir Prepared . . . and pre
sented . . . at the Celebration of the Completion of the New Yor|
Canals*, remarked that "no one can say how far we owe this occasion
to the ability with which [Colles] developed the great advantages tha
would result from opening the communications with the Lakes." [31]

Writing some eight decades after Colles' death, John Mines recalled
that in St. Paul's "churchyard a . . . native of Ireland is interred whe
. . . did more for the practical benefit of his fellowman and more fo
the public prosperity of New York than any other who sleeps in the
enclosure. This was Christopher Collis [*sic*]." [32]

In his Memoir honoring Governor DeWitt Clinton, Dr. David
Hosack confirmed that "Christopher Colles . . . was the first person
who suggested to the government of the state, the canals and improve
ments on the Ontario route." [33] This was seconded by J. A. Stevens who
attested that "to no single individual is the system of American im
provements more indebted than to Christopher Colles." [34]

In a eulogy to Dr. John W. Francis published in 1866, Benson J
Lossing remembered that he had "often heard [Francis] speak in
dignantly of the neglect in life, and forgetfulness after death, o
Christopher Colles, one of the brightest and most far-seeing men ir
our country two generations back. . . . His name is but little knowr

[30] Henry O'Rielly, "Material for Telegraph History," p. 262.
[31] Colden, *Memoir* (New York, 1825), p. 21.
[32] Mines, *Walks*, p. 137.
[33] Hosack, *Memoir of DeWitt Clinton*, p. 281.
[34] J. A. Stevens, "Christopher Colles," *Magazine of American History*, II (1878)
340.

o this generation, while the influence of his genius is everywhere felt
n the great pulsating arteries of our national enterprise." [35]

To compensate for the "neglect in life," Dr. Francis published
n 1855 a lengthy treatise entitled "Reminiscences of Christopher
Colles." [36] In it he observed that Colles "long bore a conspicuous part
n the affairs of our active population, and whose life and trials may
be set forth as an instructive instance of personal warfare against
conflicting elements." [37] Despite the many adversities encountered
during the long lifetime of his versatile friend, Francis acknowledged
that "there were enough enlightened minds and generous hearts to
recognize the merits of Colles." [38]

We can conclude, therefore, that in the judgment of history, the
career of Christopher Colles was one of notable achievement. His
many ideas and projects, and their far-reaching effects, long outlived
the visionary little man with the "sparse white locks [and the] cavernous gray eyes." That judgment has been summed up in our day by
Greville Bathe, who states that "of the many men who contributed
their scientific and philosophical knowledge to the advancement of
American culture, both before and after the Revolution, few can claim
more distinction than Christopher Colles." [39]

[35] Quoted by Henry T. Tuckerman in biographical sketch of Francis in the
latter's *Old New York*, pp. cxxvi–cxxvii.
[36] Francis, "Reminiscences of Colles."
[37] *Ibid.*, p. 197.
[38] *Ibid.*, p. 206.
[39] Bathe, *An Engineer's Miscellany*, p. 117.

# X

# The *Survey of the Roads*, Contemporary Guidebook and Historical Record

I~N~ evaluating Christopher Colles' road book it is necessary to consider first its utility in the period when it was published, and secondly, its significance as a historical document today. When the first plates of the *Survey* were distributed in 1789, the infant nation was still struggling to lift itself out of the post-war economic depression, and was about to inaugurate its president and seat the first Congress under the newly adopted Constitution.

The former thirteen colonies, whose interests had been economically and traditionally oriented to England before the war, were now, as part of the Federal union, faced with the problem of establishing relations and communications with their sister states. Of vital importance was an effective transportation network.

Prior to 1750, the colonists were dependent, almost exclusively, upon water transportation. Settlements, with few exceptions, were along the coast, on the shores of enclosed bays, or along the lower courses of rivers that flowed into the sea. Such land travel as there was between the several colonies was made on horseback along paths that, in many instances, followed Indian trails.

So unimportant was land transportation that it was not until 1729 that a map of America showing roads was published. By the middle of the eighteenth century a few short distance stage lines were in operation, often as links or "land ferries" connecting water routes across necks of land.

There were attempts in the seventeen forties to establish a stage line between Philadelphia and New York, but the service over this route was not regular until 1756. The journey between the two cities initially required three days, which was reduced to two by 1766.

ive years later newspaper advertisements heralded Mercereau's "Flying Machine" stage with a travel time of only a day and a half between New York and Philadelphia.

Although there was some stage coach development in New England and in the southern states before the Revolution, it was impossible to travel by stage without interruption the full extent of the colonies from north to south.

Intermittent staging continued during the Revolutionary War in some few localities. Regularly scheduled travel was, however, virtually nonexistent during these years. The war emphasized to military commanders, as well as to the soldiers of the Continental Army, the importance of improved roads.

With peace and reconstruction, public transportation needs became even more urgent. This was particularly true for New York City, the temporary seat of the Federal Government. Regular stage service was, therefore, reestablished between Philadelphia and New York in 1783 (Fig. 29). The following year scheduled lines were operating to New York from Boston and Richmond, Virginia, and by 1786 there was a stage line from Albany to the Federal capital.

Roads remained in wretched condition, however, and travel over them was a hazardous venture as well as a rigorous endurance test (Fig. 30). Neither the young states nor the shaky Federal government could spare funds for road building or improvement. To aggravate the financial situation, the post-war economic depression set in in 1784 and continued for three or four years. Not until 1787 did the struggling young republic begin to extricate itself from the economic mire.

Adoption of the Constitution was a psychological spur to recovery. During the war a number of industries had developed, and the interchange of agricultural and industrial goods between the states increased in volume each year. Before the Revolution the colonists, with some few exceptions, lived in rural areas. By 1790, the development of commerce and industry had resulted in increased urban residence. The normal growth in population, plus accelerated immigration, had expanded settlement throughout lower New England, New York State southeast of Fort Stanwix, the southern half of Pennsylvania, and the present limits of Virginia and the two Carolinas. Venturesome souls were even pushing across the Appalachians into the Ohio valley. The

97

Fig. 29. Philadelphia was an important stage center on one of the major routes shown in the *Survey of the Roads*. The "Stage Waggon" here pictured is an improved version of coaches in service shortly after the Revolution. From Charles W. Janson, *The Stranger in America*, 1807. Courtesy of the Library of Congress.

Fig. 30. The unsurfaced roads and rural landscape of southeastern Pennsylvania are well portrayed in this 1788 view. From *Columbian Magazine*, July 1788. Courtesy of the Library of Congress.

Fig. 31. On his triumphal journey from Mount Vernon to New York City for his inauguration as the first President of the United States, George Washington traveled over roads mapped in Colles' *Survey*. Gray's Ferry, here shown decorated in Washington's honor, crossed the Schuylkill River just south of Philadelphia. From *Columbian Magazine*, May 1789. Courtesy of the Library of Congress.

Fig. 32. Trenton was also decorated to welcome the procession of President-elect Washington in April 1789. The road here shown is on Plate 45 in Colles' road book. From *Columbian Magazine*, May 1789. Courtesy of the Library of Congress.

1790 census of the United States revealed a population of abou█ 4,000,000.

The first Congress convened in New York's Federal Hall on Marc█ 4, 1789. However, "owing to the exigencies of travel," a quorum ha█ not yet assembled. It was not until April 6 that enough members wer█ present to elect George Washington president and John Adams vice president. Three more weeks passed before the Chief Executive wa█ able to arrange his affairs and negotiate the long journey from Moun█ Vernon to New York (Figs. 31 & 32).

The year 1789 was an eventful one for the new constitutional re█ public and for New York City, its temporary capital. "Great event█ [were] on the march . . . [and] a fresh invigorating spirit [stirred] the land." [1] Almost unnoticed among the more exciting events was th█ publication of the first part of a guidebook of the country's roads█ Its compiler was a visionary engineer and scientist named Christophe█ Colles. While engaged in surveying and mapping during the Revo lution, he had anticipated a great increase in travel and commerc█ after the war, and a resulting need for good maps of the roads. Th█ surveys, as he stated in the broadside announcing the guidebook, wer█ "made from actual mensuration, by a perambulator of a new and con venient construction, invented [by himself] . . . which determine█ the number of revolutions of a wheel of a carriage to which it is fixed." [2]

The enterprising publisher was enthusiastic about the potential use fulness of his *Survey of the Roads.* In it, he announced,

> . . . a traveller will . . . find so plain and circumstantial a descriptio█ of the road, that whilst he has the draft with him it will be impossible fo█ him to miss his way: he will have the satisfaction of knowing the names o█ many of the persons who reside on the road; . . . If a foreigner arrives i█ any part of the Continent and is under the necessity to travel by land, h█ applies to a bookseller, who with the assistance of the index map chooses ou█ the particular pages which are necessary for his direction. It is expected [concluded the author of the guide, that] many other entertaining and use ful purposes will be discovered when these surveys come into general use." [3]

To Colles it seemed that the *Survey of the Roads* would be a sure-

[1] Frank Monaghan and Marvin Lowenthal, *This Was New York, the Nation's Capital in 1789* (Garden City, N. Y., 1943), p. v.
[2] Colles, *Proposals for Publishing.*
[3] *Ibid.*

re best seller. Unfortunately, the demand he hoped for did not develop, and within a year or two publication of the incompleted series of maps was halted, to the great disappointment and financial loss of its compiler. A number of factors probably contributed to the failure of the *Survey.*

Monaghan and Lowenthal, in their entertaining and informative book entitled *This Was New York, the Nation's Capital, in 1789,* described some of the difficulties and problems a traveler faced in undertaking a journey from Boston to New York:

> Setting out on [such a journey], you consulted first of all not a timetable but a calendar. You reckoned on . . . not less than six days from Boston to New York]. . . . If you decided to head for Manhattan by land, you had the choice of driving your own chaise or taking the stages. In the first instance you did wisely if you bought a copy of that handy little book, Christopher Colles' *Survey of the Roads of the United States of America,* which appeared in 1789.[4]

Few persons at this time could afford the luxury of a private chaise. Public stage lines were the common carriers in 1789, and most cross-country travelers patronized them (Fig. 33). Individual voyagers had little occasion to consult route maps, for they trusted the stage driver to guide them to their destination. At the speed the stages operated between 25 and 60 miles per day, depending upon the weather and road conditions) there was little danger of getting lost. There were few crossroads, and, moreover, it called for little knowledge of navigation or cartography to guide the horses along the deeply rutted main highways. The stretch of road or "stage" covered by one coach was usually around twenty miles, so the drivers were thoroughly familiar with every cultural and topographical detail along the way. The rough, though skilled, stage drivers probably would have scorned the suggestion that they needed a road map.

Colles looked also to foreign visitors as potential users of his *Survey.* This class of traveler was quite numerous and should have constituted good market for the guide book. Peace was hardly established before Europeans with various objectives and interests flocked to America. Some came to look over the new republic and report on its geography, institutions, and progress to their countrymen. Others saw in the young

[4] Monaghan and Lowenthal, *This Was New York,* p. 2.

101

Fig. 33. A "Stage Waggon," loaded with travelers, departs from a roadside tavern on the next stage of its journey. Note the proximity of forest to the road and tavern, tree stumps in the cleared fields, and the unsurfaced road. From Weld's *Travels through the States of North America . . . 1795, 1796, and 1797,* London, 1800. Courtesy of the Library of Congress.

and financially weak nation a promising field for investment. The books, journals, diaries, newspaper articles, and letters written by these visitors constitute a rich source of information for the first several decades following adoption of the Constitution.

An examination of a number of the published accounts, however, reveals no mention of the use of Colles' *Survey of the Roads,* nor even any reference to the existence of such a publication. Promotion and distribution problems were formidable, and, while foreign visitors undoubtedly would have found the guide useful, few apparently were aware of its existence. In fact, less than twenty years after the *Survey* was issued, Mathew Carey of Philadelphia, in the preface to Moore and Jones' *Traveller's Directory,* published by his firm, stated that "repeated demands for an American Book of Roads by native as well as foreign Travellers, have induced me to publish this Directory." [5]

[5] S. S. Moore and T. W. Jones, *The Traveller's Directory or a Pocket Companion* (Philadelphia, 1802).

102

In all probability for the reasons here cited, few copies of the *Survey of the Roads* were purchased for use as guide books. Colles' work, however, is known to have been in the private libraries of a number of prominent persons of the period. An exhibit at the John Carter Brown Library in 1949, entitled "The Colonial Scene 1602–1800," included a copy of the *Survey.* The catalog of the exhibit described the *Survey* as "one of the most generally useful books of the post-Revolutionary period in the United States." [6]

In potential utility the road book certainly merited this appraisal. Actually, however, the country and its citizens were not yet ready for a guide of this type and quality.

Although Colles' guide book was not appreciated by his contemporaries, it stands today as one of the most valuable historical records of the United States for the Revolutionary War years and those immediately following. It is not only the earliest American road book, but ranks also as one of the first private map publishing ventures.

Some years ago, the late Ralph H. Brown observed that:

. . . the year 1800 roughly marks the mid-point of a twenty year period remarkable for the content and coverage of contemporary geographical materials. This material . . . [is] amplified by many maps of great variety — tangible evidence of a widespread interest in things geographical.[7]

He noted further that:

. . . the distinguishing feature of the maps is the cartographic break with the past which they represent. The maps of larger significance were made by map-makers not by map-copiers. Consequently there is a minimum of carry-over from post-Revolutionary maps to those prepared or published at the opening of the next century. Map making during this period is linked with certain individuals who compiled much new data, some of which they themselves secured.[8]

In the vanguard of these individuals was Christopher Colles. As we have seen, some of the maps in the *Survey* were based upon data derived from personal surveys. For the remainder of the plates he

[6] "The Colonial Scene 1602–1800. . . ," in *American Antiquarian Society: Proceedings* (April 19–Oct. 18, 1950), p. 141.
[7] Ralph H. Brown, "Materials Bearing Upon the Geography of the Atlantic Seaboard, 1790 to 1810," in *Association of American Geographers: Annals,* vol. 28 (Sept. 1938), p. 206.
[8] *Ibid.,* pp. 226–227.

103

utilized the original and unpublished maps made by the geographers of the Continental Army. Few contemporary documents preserve for us the comprehensive detail that is recorded in Colles' *Survey of the Roads of the United States of America.*

It traces first of all the primary transportation routes for a large segment of the country. Inasmuch as most habitations were immediately adjacent to the roads, the maps in the guide book reveal the basic settlement pattern of the period.

Particularly valuable to historians, genealogists, and social scientists are the 800 names of geographical features, community and cultural centers, industrial establishments, and individual home owners. In the road book one can locate the residences of such distinguished early Americans as Generals Washington, Schuyler, and Montgomery, Governor Livingston, Lieutenant-Governor Cortlandt, and the Brevoorts, Rhinelanders, and Roosevelts. Also accurately set down are the homesteads of some less renowned families, such as the Dales, Hopkins, Jones, Johnsons, Millers, and Smiths (Fig. 34).

It is regretted that Colles, except in rare instances, did not include given names or initials of the inhabitants. For some individuals such more positive identification may be found on the manuscript Erskine-DeWitt maps in the collections of the New-York Historical Society.

Representative industrial and commercial establishments identified in the *Survey* are pottery plants, iron works, warehouses, stores, and boring, flax, fulling, saw, and tub, and, of course, numerous grist mills (Fig. 35). Thirty-five of the latter are located.

In the *Proposals,* Colles recognized the importance of blacksmith shops to the traveler in the event "his horse should want a shoe, or his carriage be broke," and some two dozen are shown. Taverns and inns were essential to travelers whose "stages" averaged only 20 miles. Accordingly they were liberally strung along the highways, and provided rest, shelter, and food for the passengers as well as for the stage coach driver and his horses. Some 160 taverns are located in the *Survey of the Roads,* probably only a fraction of those in operation. For in addition to serving itinerant Americans and foreign visitors, inns were also centers of social life and community activity. Only a few of the urban taverns are shown in the guide book.

The legend has distinctive symbols for Episcopal and Presbyterian

104

Fig. 34. A farmstead on a dirt road in northern New Jersey is pictured in this scene. From *New York Magazine*, June 1794. Courtesy of the Library of Congress.

Fig. 35. Grist mills were common along American roads in Colles' day. This scene is on Plate 40 in the *Survey of the Roads*. From *New York Magazine*, November 1794. Courtesy of the Library of Congress.

churches, and the maps locate 19 of the former and 21 of the latter. Several other denominations are noticed and identified, including a Quaker Meeting House, and Baptist and Sandemanian churches. Educational institutions on Colles' maps include seven schools, one academy, and two colleges (Princeton, and William and Mary). Only five doctors are recognized by name and title.

In his *Proposals for Publishing a Survey of the Roads*, Colles indicated that the completed work would include "alphabetical lists [and] other necessary explanation of the drafts," as well as "a set of general maps . . . upon a small scale . . . [which] will . . . answer as an index." These features were never completed or incorporated in the *Survey* because of its premature demise.

An index map, locating the 83 plates, and alphabetical name indexes, both comprehensive and classified, are included in this reprint edition. These reference aids greatly enhance the utility of the *Survey of the Roads* as a primary record for the first decades of the history of the United States.

# Bibliography of Christopher Colles

COLLES, CHRISTOPHER. *An Account of the Astonishing Beauties and Operations of Nature, in the Minute Creation, Displayed by the Solar Microscope.* New York: printed and sold by Samuel Wood, at the Juvenile Bookstore, no. 357 Pearl Street, 1815. 44 pp.

———— Broadside announcing public lecture on the telegraph. Oct. 1812.

———— *Description of the Numerical Telegraph. For Communicating Unexpected Intelligence by Figures, Letters, Words and Sentences.* Brooklyn: Spooner, 1813. 19 pp.

———— *The Geographical Ledger and Systematized Atlas, . . . by Christopher Colles of New York.* Printed by John Buel, No. 24, Little Q Street, New York, 1794.

———— *Proposal . . . . for Furnishing the City of New York with a Constant Supply of Fresh Water.* New York: printed by Hugh Gaine, 1774. Broadside, 15 x 9½ inches.

———— *Proposal of a Design for the Promotion of the Interests of the United States of America, Extending its Advantages to All Ranks and Conditions of men . . . by Means of Inland Navigable Communications of a New Construction and Mode. . . .* New York: printed for the author by Samuel Wood, no. 362 Pearl Street, 1808. 22 pp.

———— *Proposals for Publishing a Survey of the Roads of the United States of America.* New York: c. 1789. Broadside, 11½ x 7¾ inches. Two states. Second state has additional line at bottom reading: "Subscription papers will be sent to most of the booksellers on the continent."

———— *Proposals for the Speedy Settlement of the Waste and Unappropriated Lands on the Western Frontiers of the State of New York, and for the Improvement of the Inland Navigation Between Albany and Oswego.* New York: Samuel Loudon, 1785. 14 pp.

———— *Shortly will be Published An Account of the Astonishing Beauties and Operations of Nature in the Minute Creation. . . By the Solar Microscope.* New York: 1812. Broadside.

———— *A Survey of the Roads of the United States of America.* New York: 1789-[1792].

———— *Syllabus of a Course of Lectures in Natural Experimental Philosophy, by Christopher Colles.* Philadelphia: printed by John Dunlap, c. 1773. Broadside.

# General Bibliography

*American Archives: A Collection of Authentick Records . . . The Whole Forming A Documentary History of the Origin and Growth of the North American Colonies,* ed. PETER FORCE. Fifth ser., vol. 3. Washington, D. C.: 1853.

*American Scenic and Historic Preservation Society: Seventeenth Annual Report, 1912.* Albany, N. Y.: 1912.

*American Scenic and Historic Preservation Society: Nineteenth Annual Report, 1914.* Albany, N. Y.: 1914.

*American Philosophical Society: Early Proceedings of the American Philosophical Society . . . from the Manuscript Minutes of its Meetings from 1744 to 1838.* Philadelphia: 1884.

*American State Papers: Class 7, Post Office Department, Documents Legislative and Executive of the Congress of the United States 1789 to 1833,* selected and ed. by Walter Lowrie and Walter S. Franklin. Washington: U. S. Government Printing Office, 1834.

BATHE, GREVILLE. *An Engineer's Miscellany.* Philadelphia: Patterson & White, 1938. 136 pp.

BAYLES, W. HARRISON. *Old Taverns of New York.* New York: Frank Allaben, 1915. 489 pp.

BECK, T. Romeyn. *Eulogium on Simeon DeWitt.* Albany, N. Y.: Albany Institute, Apr. 23, 1835.

BISHOP, J. LEANDER. *A History of American Manufactures from 1608 to 1860.* Philadelphia: Edward Young, 1868. 3 vols.

BROWN, RALPH H. "Materials Bearing Upon the Geography of the Atlantic Seaboard, 1790 to 1810," *Association of American Geographers: Annals,* vol. 28 (Sept. 1938), pp. 201–231.

——— *Mirror for Americans, Likeness of the Eastern Seaboard, 1810.* New York: American Geographical Society, 1943. 312 pp.

CALLAHAN, NORTH. *Henry Knox, General Washington's General.* New York: Rinehart, 1958. 404 pp.

CARMAN, HARRY J. "The Professions in New York in 1800," *Columbia University Quarterly,* vol. 23 (June, 1931), pp. 159–175.

CHURCH, ELIHU D. *A Catalogue of Books Relating to the Discovery and Early History of North and South America. Forming a Part of the Library of E. D. Church,* compiled and annotated by GEORGE WATSON COLE, vol. 5 (1753–1884). New York: Peter Smith, 1951.

COLDEN, CADWALLADER D. *Memoir Prepared at the Request of a Committee of the Common Council of the City of New York and Pre-*

sented to the Mayor of the City at the Celebration of the Completing o
the New York Canals. New York: printed by order of the Corporation o
New York, by W. A. Davis, 1825. 408 pp.

COLLES, CHRISTOPER J. "Ancestry of Christopher Colles in Ireland,
in American Irish Historical Society: Journal, vol. 29 (1931), pp. 67–71

"The Colonial Scene 1602–1800. An Annotated List of Books, Broadsides
Prints, and Maps . . . Based on an Exhibit at John Carter Brow
Library in May, 1949," in American Antiquarian Society: Proceedings
vol. 60 (Apr. 19, 1950–Oct. 18, 1950), pp. 53–160.

The Columbian Magazine. New York: issue of July 1816.

The Daily Advertiser. New York: Francis Childs and (after July 1789) Joh
Swaine, issues of May 1, 1786, and Aug. 1, 1789.

DEFOREST, EMILY. James Colles, 1788–1883. New York: privatel
printed, 1926. 295 pp.

DEFOREST, THEODORE R. "Water Chronology of the City of Nev
York," in D. T. VALENTINE, Manual of the Corporation of the Cit
of New York for 1854 (New York, 1854), pp. 214–223.

DICKSON, HAROLD E. John Wesley Jarvis, American Painter, 1780–184C
New York: New-York Historical Society, 1949, 476 pp.

DOYLE, RICHARD D. "Christopher Colles, Engineer and Philosopher,
Historical Bulletin (Chicago: Loyola U. P.), vol. 9 (Mar. 1931), pp. 47
49.

Dunlap's Pennsylvania Packet. Philadelphia: John Dunlap, issues of Feb
ruary 17, 1772, and September 22, 1773.

DWIGHT, TIMOTHY. Travels in New-England and New-York, vol. I
New Haven: Dwight, 1821.

Facts and Observations in Relation to the Origin and Completion of th
Erie Canal. Providence, R.I.: Carlile and Brown, 2nd edit., 1827. 32 pp

FERRAR, J. The History of Limerick . . . to the Year 1787. . . . Limerick
1787.

FORDHAM, HERBERT G. John Ogilby (1600–1676), His Brittania an
the British Itineraries of the Eighteenth Century. London: Oxford U. P
1925. 21 pp.

FRANCIS, JOHN W. New York During the Last Half Century. New York
John Trow, 1857. 232 pp.

———— Old New York, a Reminiscence of the Past Sixty Years, With
Memoir of the Author by Henry T. Tuckerman. New York: Middleto
1866.

———— "Reminiscences of Christopher Colles," in Knickerbocker Galler
(New York: 1855), pp. 189–208.

FREEMAN, DOUGLAS SOUTHALL. George Washington, a Biograph
vol. 5. New York: Scribners, 1952.

The Freeman's Journal, or North American Intelligencer. Philadelphia

Francis Bailey, issue of Mar. 10, 1790, and intermittent issues to Oct. 6, 1790.

GOFF, FREDERICK R. "The First Decade of the Federal Act for Copyright, 1790–1800," in *Essays Honoring Lawrence C. Wroth* (Portland, Maine: 1951), pp. 101–128.

GOTTESMAN, RITA S. *The Arts and Crafts in New York, 1726–1776.* New York: New-York Historical Society, 1938.

GRIFFIN, LLOYD W. "Christopher Colles and His Two American Map Series," in *Bibliographical Society of America: Papers,* vol. 48 (1954), pp. 170–182.

HALL, EDWARD HAGAMAN. "The Catskill Aqueduct," chap. iv of "Early Pipe Line Projects, Christopher Colles' Water-works," in *American Scenic and Historic Preservation Society: Annual Report,* no. 23 (Albany: 1918), pp. 687–735.

—— *The Catskill Aqueduct and Earlier Water Supplies in the City of New York.* New York: the Mayor's Catskill Aqueduct Celebration Committee, 1917. 132 pp.

HARMON, A. C. "Map of Annapolis-Alexandria Road," in *Columbia Historical Society of Washington, D. C.: Records,* vols. 40 & 41 (1940), p. 226.

HAYES, LYMAN S. "The Navigation of the Connecticut River," in *Vermont Historical Society: Proceedings, 1915–1916,* pp. 49–86.

HEUSSER, ALBERT H. *The Forgotten General, Robert Erskine, F.R.S. (1735–1780).* Paterson, N.J.: Benjamin Franklin Press, 1928. 216 pp.

HOSACK, DAVID. *Memoir of DeWitt Clinton.* New York: Seymour, 1829. 560 pp.

JEFFERSON, THOMAS. *Writings,* ed. ANDREW A. LIPSCOMB, vol. 12. Washington: Thomas Jefferson Memorial Association, 1903.

KING, CHARLES. *A Memoir of the Construction, Cost, and Capacity of the Croton Aqueduct.* New York: Charles King, 1843. 308 pp.

KIRBY, RICHARD SHELTON. "Christopher Colles," in his "Some Early American Engineers and Surveyors," in *Connecticut Society of Civil Engineers: Transactions, 1930,* pp. 38–42.

—— and PHILIP GUSTAVE LAURSON. *The Early Years of Modern Civil Engineering.* New Haven: Yale U. P., 1932. 324 pp.

LAMB, JOHN. "Papers." Unpublished manuscript, New-York Historical Society.

LEAKE, ISAAC Q. *Memoir of the Life and Times of General John Lamb.* Albany: John Munsell, 1857. 431 pp.

LOSSING, BENSON J. *History of New York City.* New York: Perine, 1884. 881 pp.

LOVE, W. DELOSS. "The Navigation of the Connecticut River," in *Ameri-*

can *Antiquarian Society: Proceedings*, vol. 15 (Apr. 29, 1903), pp. 38!
441.

MARTIN, LAWRENCE. "Division of Maps," in *U. S. Library of Congres
Annual Report for the Fiscal Year Ending June 30, 1937*. Washingtor
U. S. Government Printing Office, 1937.

MINES, JOHN FLAVEL (pseud., Felix Oldboy). *Walks in Our Churc!
yards, Old New York, Trinity Parish*. New York: Geo. Gottsberger Pec!
1895. 181 pp.

MONAGHAN, FRANK and MARVIN LOWENTHAL. *This Was Ne
York, the Nation's Capital in 1789*. Garden City, N.Y.: Doubleday, 194!
308 pp.

MOORE, S. S. and T. W. JONES. *The Traveller's Directory or a Pock
Companion, Shewing the Course of the Main Road from Philadelphia t
New York and from Philadelphia to Washington*. Philadelphia: Mathe
Carey, 1802. 23 pp.

NASH, WILLIS G. "The Burning of Kingston," in *Ulster County Historic
Society: Proceedings, 1933–1934*, pp. 51–60.

*New York Gazette and General Advertiser*. New York: John Lang, issu
of Oct. 7, 1816.

*New York Gazette and Weekly Mercury*. New York: Hugh Gaine, issue
Aug. 1, 1774.

*New-York Historical Society: Proceedings, for the year 1845*. New Yor!
1846.

*New York Packet and the American Advertiser*. Fishkill, N.Y.: Samu
Loudon, issue of Aug. 30, 1781.

New York State Legislature. Assembly. *Journal*, 1784, 1785, 1786. Alban
New York State Legislature. Senate. *Journal*, 1784. Albany.

New York State. Secretary of State. *Journals of the Military Expedition
Major General John Sullivan . . . in 1779*. Auburn, N.Y.: 1887.

O'BRIEN, MICHAEL J. *In Old New York, the Irish Dead in Trinity an
St. Paul's Churchyards*. New York: American Irish Historical Societ
1928.

O'REILLY [later O'Rielly], HENRY. *Sketches of Rochester with Incident
Notices of Western New York*. Rochester: William Alling, 1838. 416 p

——— "Material for Telegraph History, II. Christopher Colles and th
First Proposal for a Telegraphy System in the United States," in *Th
Historical Magazine*, vol. 5 (Apr.–May 1869), pp. 262–269, 323, 329–33

"An Outline History of New York's Water Supply," in *New-York Historic
Society: Quarterly*, vol. 1 (Oct. 1917), pp. 63–70.

*The Pennsylvania Chronicle*. Philadelphia: William Goddard, issue of Au
26, 1771.

*The Pennsylvania Gazette*. Philadelphia: William and David Hall, an
William Sellers, issue of Sept. 29, 1773.

NTARD, JOHN. *Letters . . . to His Daughter Eliza Noel Pintard David-son*, vol. 1 (1816–1820), ed. DOROTHY C. BARCK. New York: New-York Historical Society, 1940.

'ioneer Road Maps," *Motor Travel* (Automobile Club of America), vol. 8 (June 1916), pp. 63–64.

OMERANTZ, SIDNEY I. *New York, an American City, 1783–1803.* New York: Columbia U. P., 1938. 531 pp.

RIME, ALFRED COXE. *The Arts & Crafts in Philadelphia, Maryland, and South Carolina, 1721–1785.* Walpole Society, 1929.

ivington's *New-York Gazetteer.* New York: James Rivington, issues of March 10 & 17, 1774.

UTTENBER, E. M. *Obstructions to the Navigation of Hudson's River.* Albany: Munsell, 1860. 210 pp.

CHOONMAKER, MARIUS. *History of Kingston, New York.* New York: Burr, 1888. 558 pp.

HERMAN, ANDREW M. *Historic Morristown, N.J., the Story of its First Century.* Morristown: Howard, 1905. 444 pp.

IMMS, JEPTHA R. *History of Schoharie County and the Border Wars of New York.* Albany: Munsell and Tanner, 1845. 672 pp.

MITH, THOMAS E. V. *The City of New York in the Year of Washington's Inauguration, 1789.* New York: 1889. 244 pp.

PAULDING, E. WILDER. *New York in the Critical Period, 1783–1789.* New York: Columbia U. P., 1932. 334 pp.

TAUFFER, DAVID MCNEELEY. *American Engravers Upon Copper and Steel.* 2 vols. New York: The Grolier Club, 1907. Vol. 1, 391 pp.; vol. 2, 566 pp.

TEVENS, J. A. "Christopher Colles," in *Magazine of American History*, vol. 2 (1878), pp. 340–348.

IEBOUT, CORNELIUS H. *The Ancestry and Posterity of Cornelius Henry Tiebout.* New York: private printing, 1910. 80 pp.

WINING, THOMAS. *Travels in America 100 Years Ago.* New York: Harper, 1894. 281 pp.

. S. Congress. House. *Journal of the House of Representatives of the United States*, First and Second Congress, 1789–1793. Washington: 1826. 831 pp.

. S. Continental Congress. *Journals of the Continental Congress, 1774–1789.* Edited from the original records in the Library of Congress. 34 vols. Washington: U. S. Government Printing Office, 1904–1937.

ERPLANCK, GULIAN C. "Reminiscences of New York, no. II," in *The Talisman for 1830* (New York: Elam Bliss, 1829), pp. 337–358.

'ASHINGTON, GEORGE. *Letters . . . to George and James Clinton, a Collection of Thirty-five Letters, of Which Twenty-Six are Unpublished, Together With Washington's War Map of New York and New Jersey.*

113

New York: jointly owned and offered for sale by George H. Richmon
and by the New York Cooperative Society, 1934. 72 pp.
—— "Papers." Vol. 214, 1783 (Jan. 7–Jan. 26). Unpublished manuscrip
Library of Congress, Manuscript Division.
—— *The Writings of George Washington From the Original Manuscrip
Sources, 1745–1799* . . . , ed. JOHN C. FITZPATRICK. 39 vol
Washington: U. S. Government Printing Office, 1931–1944.
WEGMANN, EDWARD. *The Water-supply of the City of New York 1658
1895.* New York: Wiley, 1896. 316 pp.
WESTCOTT, THOMPSON. *Life of John Fitch, the Inventor of the Steam
boat.* Philadelphia: Lippincott, 1878. 428 pp.
WHITFORD, NOBLE E. *History of the Canal System of the State of
New York Together With Brief Histories of the Canals of the Unite
States and Canada,* Supplement to the Annual Report of the State Eng
neer and Surveyor . . . for the . . . Year Ending September 30, 190.
Albany: Brandow, 1906. 1025 pp.
WILSON, JAMES GRANT. *Memorial History of New York State,* vol. ·
New York: 1893.
WRIGHT, ALBERT HAZEN. *The Sullivan Expedition of 1779.* Ithaca: th
Author, 1943.

# Inventory of Extant Copies of Colles'
## *Survey of the Roads of the United States*

No available data indicate the number of copies of Colles' *Survey* that were printed. The total for the several distributions probably was not large, and may have comprised at most several hundred copies.

Subscriptions and sales of separate sheets did not apparently exhaust the initial printing. As has been noted, the *Geographical Ledger*, presented by Colles in 1794, was to have included plates originally prepared for the *Survey*. Failure of the *Ledger* project several years after work on the *Survey* was discontinued probably found Colles still in possession of stocks of both publications. No doubt they were ultimately disposed of as waste paper.

Such copies of the road book as were acquired by travelers were very likely consulted frequently by their owners. As is the fate of road maps today, they were probably cast aside after they had served their purpose or when the pages had become worn and dog-eared.

We have observed previously that a number of political and scientific leaders of the period purchased the *Survey* for their personal libraries. These copies, in some cases specially bound, were better preserved, and several are among those extant today.

An inventory of known copies of Colles' *Survey of the Roads* was made as part of the present study. Some sixty American libraries, both public and private, were canvassed. The returns reveal fourteen complete copies (i.e., with title page and 83 plates) and nine copies lacking from one to sixty-six plates.

The maps in the *Survey* are numbered consecutively from one to 86, with the addition of numbers 45°, 46°, and 47°. Numbers 34 to 39 are not found in any copies, and undoubtedly were never issued. The following libraries report copies containing all the known plates plus a title page:

Boston Athenaeum, Boston, Mass.
Brown University, John Carter Brown Library, Providence, R. I.
Dartmouth College Library, Hanover, N. H.
Henry E. Huntington Library, San Marino, Cal.
Historical Society of Pennsylvania, Philadelphia, Pa.
Library of Congress, Map Division (2 copies), Washington, D. C.
New-York Historical Society (2 copies), New York City
New York Public Library, Rare Book Division, New York City
New York State Library, Albany, N. Y.
University of Virginia, Tracy W. McGregor Library, Charlottesville, Va.

Williams College, Chapin Library, Williamstown, Mass.
Yale University Library, New Haven, Conn.
Incomplete copies are held by the following institutions:
American Antiquarian Society, Worcester, Mass.
  Lacks title page and plates 47, 62–67, and 75–86.
American Geographical Society, New York City.
  Lacks plates 4, 17, 46°, 47°, and 68.
Columbia University Libraries, Department of Special Collections, New
  York City.
  Lacks plates 58, 60, 66, 67, 70, 72, 82, 86.
Connecticut Historical Society, Hartford, Conn.
  Lacks plate 68.
Connecticut State Library, Hartford, Conn.
  Includes only title page and plates 1 through 17.
Library Company of Philadelphia, Philadelphia, Pa.
  Lacks plates 81–86.
New Jersey Historical Society, Newark, N. J.
  Lacks title page.
New-York Historical Society, New York City.
  Has two complete copies. Third copy lacks plates 75–86.
William L. Clements Library, University of Michigan, Ann Arbor, Mich.
  Lacks plate 86.

A broadside entitled "Proposals for Publishing a Survey of the Roads
of the United States of America by Christopher Colles of New York" was
distributed with the first several maps in 1789 or early 1790. The broadside
is bound with, or inserted in, a number of the reported copies of the *Survey*.
There are two states of the sheet. On the later one there is printed at
the bottom, "Subscription papers will be sent to most of the Booksellers
on the continent." This notation is inscribed in manuscript on a copy of
the earlier state of the broadside that is in the collections of the New-York
Historical Society. The first state also lacks the paragraph stating that the
"surveys are made from actual mensuration by a perambulator of a new
and convenient construction, invented by said Colles."

PART TWO

# FACSIMILE OF CHRISTOPHER COLLES'

*Survey of the Roads*

*of the*

*United States of America, 1789*

# A SURVEY

of the

## Roads

of the

# UNITED STATES

of

*by Christopher Colles.*

### 1789

## REFERENCES.

| | | | |
|---|---|---|---|
| Episcopal Church | ☩ | Tavern | Γ |
| Presbyterian Do | ⚔ | Blacksmith Shop | ⌒ |
| Town House | ○ | Bridges mark'd by the | |
| Mill (for Grist)Except | | Road cutting the River | ⤫ |
| otherwise mark'd | ✳ | God | # |

*Scale of one Mile.*

C.Tiebout Sculp.

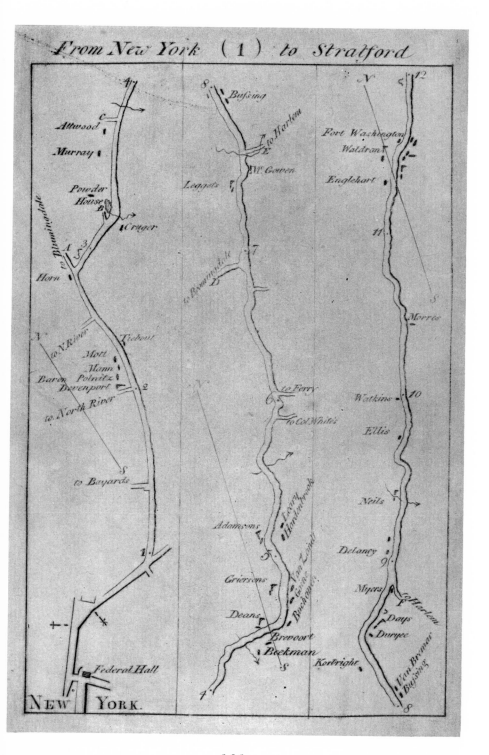

NEW YORK.

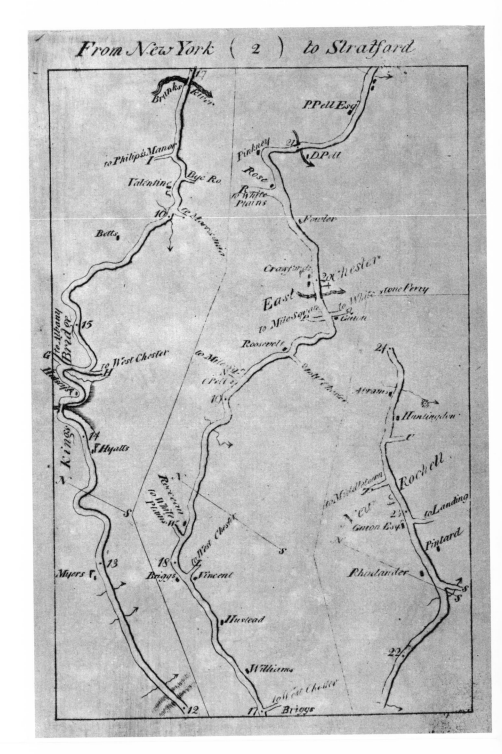

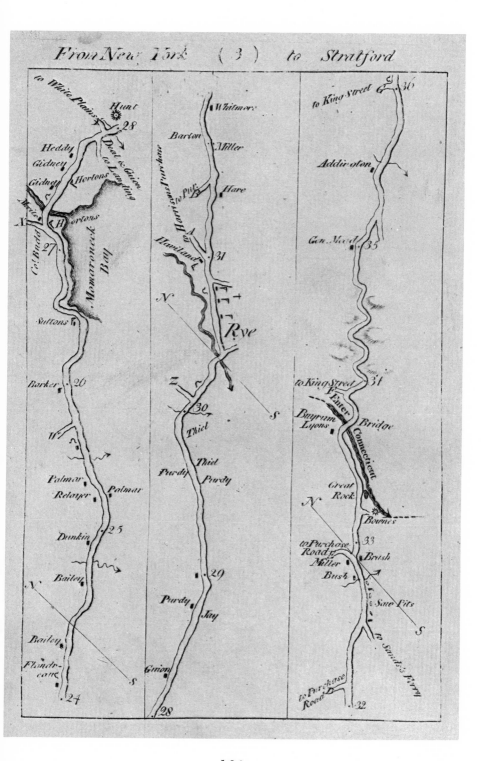

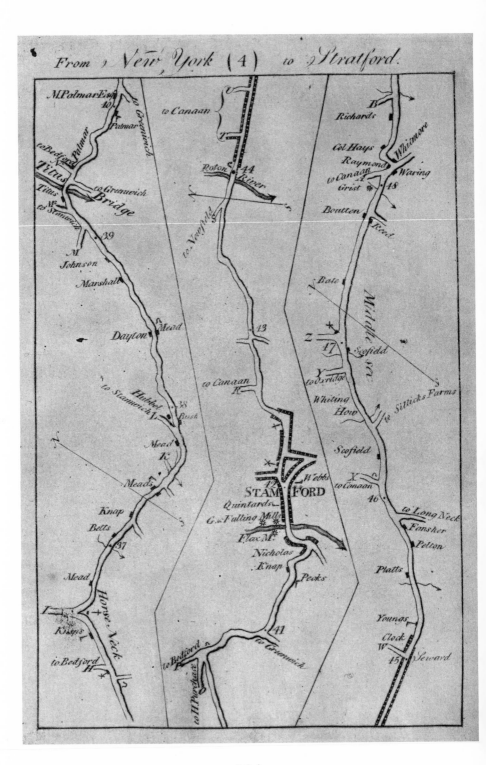

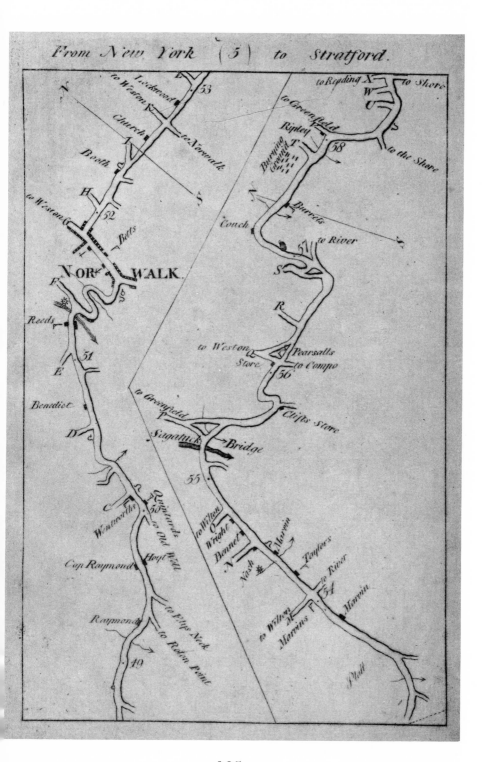

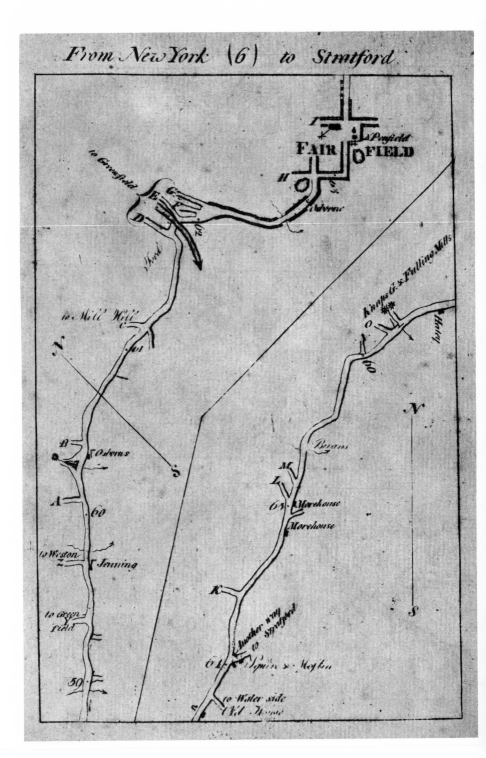

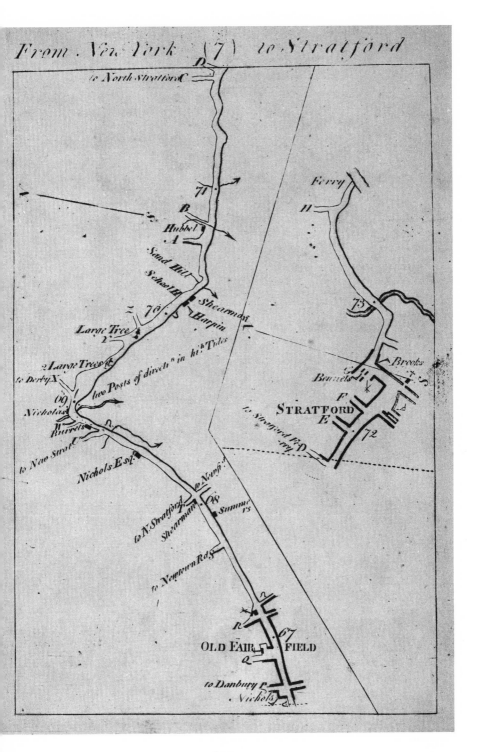

From New York (7) to Stratford

to North Stratford C

Ferry
H

71

B
Hubbel
A

Sand Hill
School H.
73

76        Shearman
Harpin

Large Tree
2

2 Large Trees

to Derby X        two Posts of directn in ht. Tides        Brooks

69                        Bennets        S
Nicholas                        F
Burrets                STRATFORD
to New Strat.                        E        72

Nichols Esqr.        to Stamford Fe D.

to N. Stratford T.
Shearman 68
Summers

to Newtown Rd.

R
OLD FAIR        67        FIELD
Q

to Danbury r.
Nichols.

127

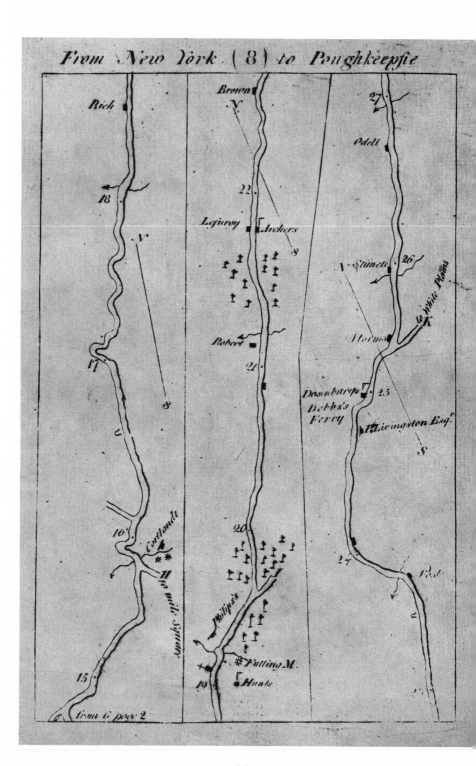

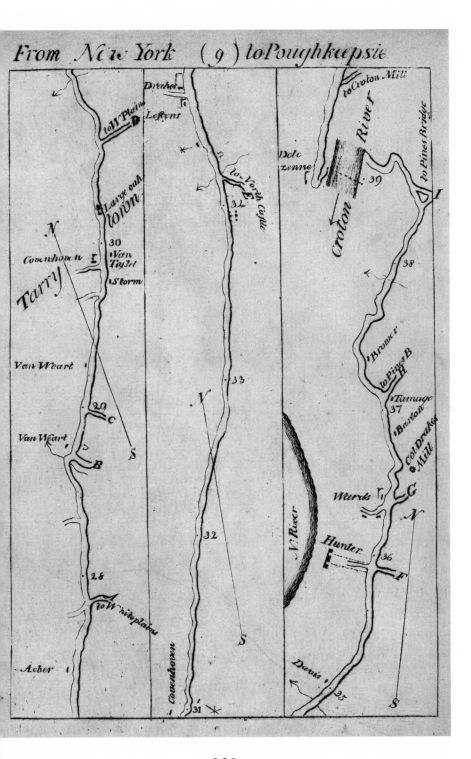

129

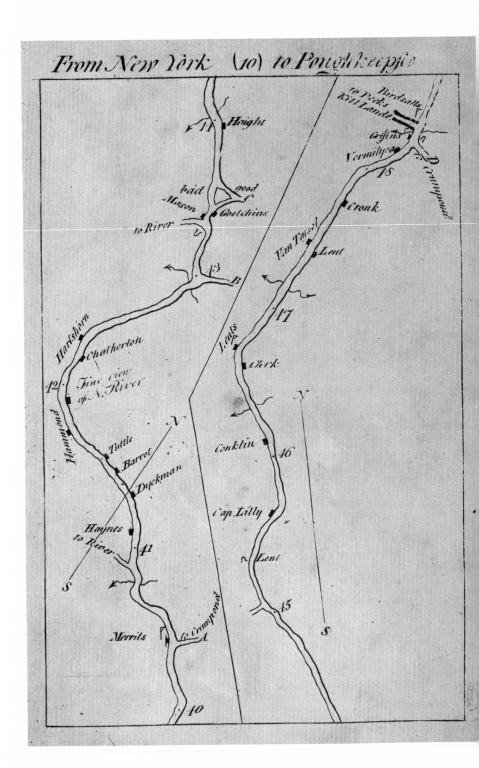

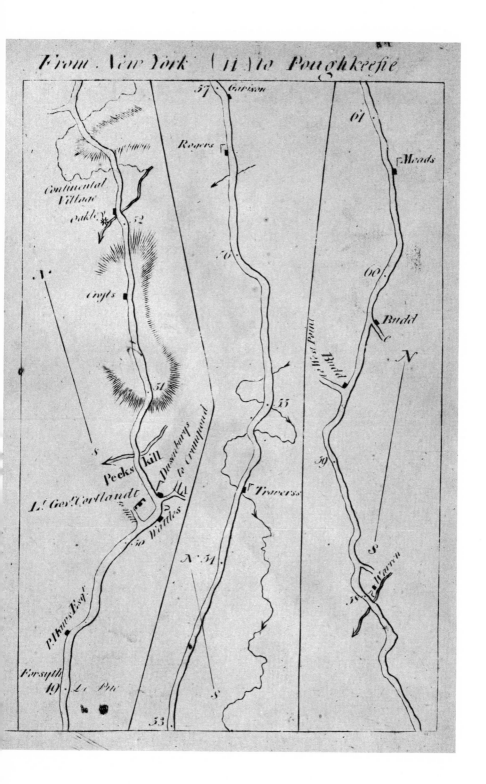

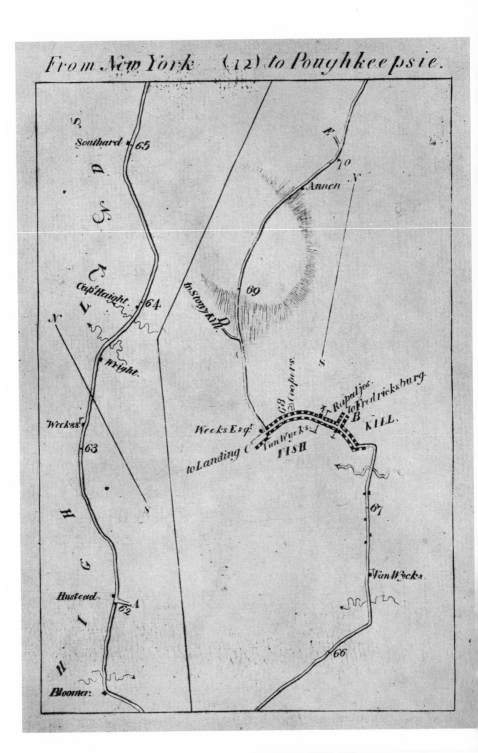

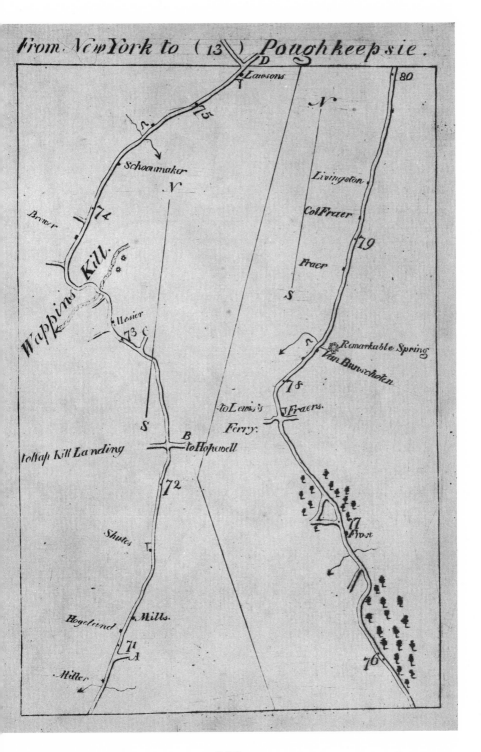

From Poughkeepsie (14) to Albany.

134

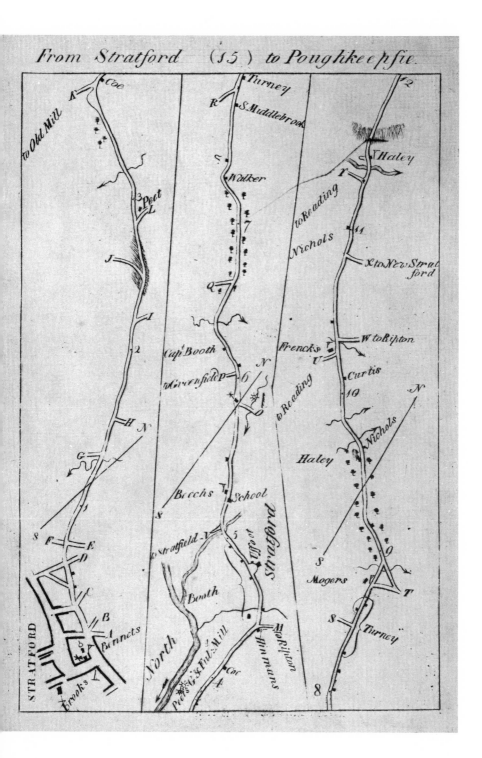

From Stratford (16) to Poughkeepsie.

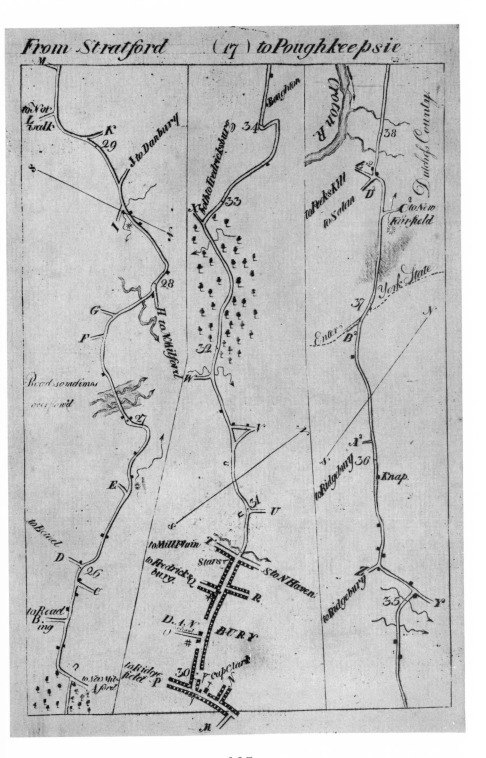

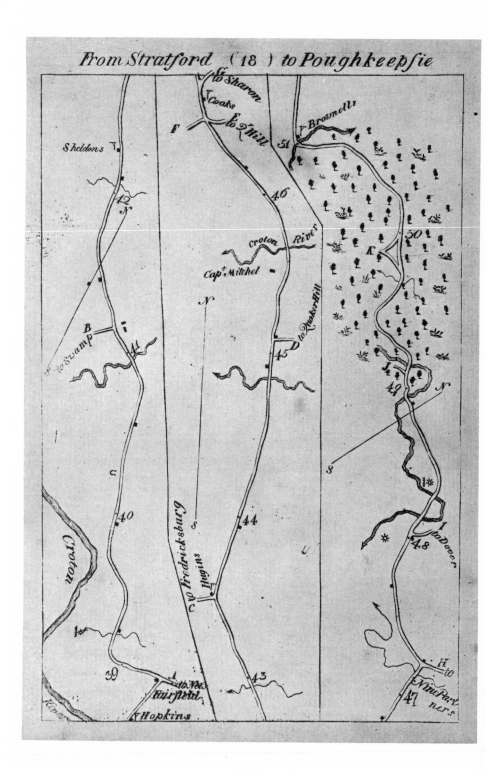

138

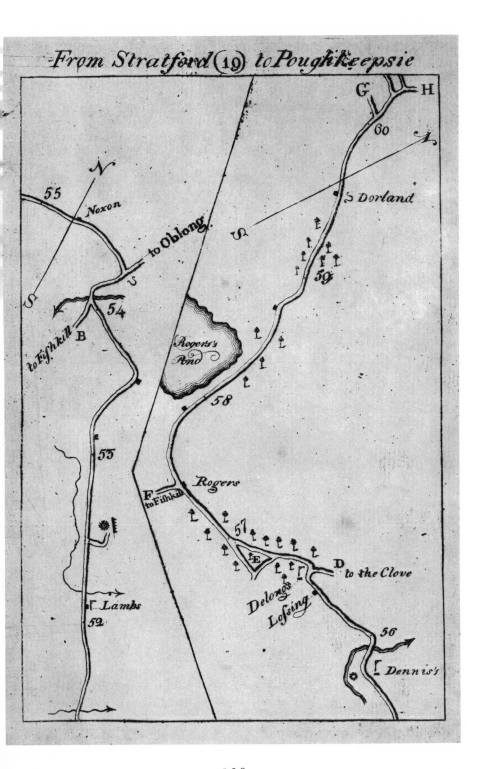

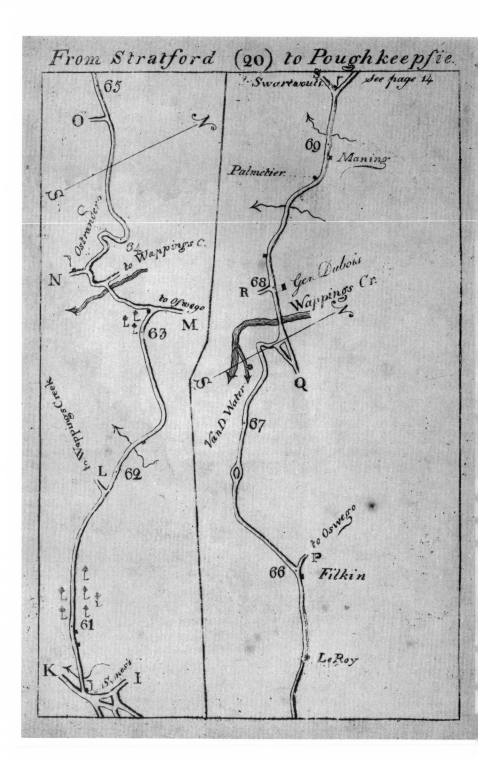

From Stratford (20) to Poughkeepsie.

65

O

S

Swartwouli    See page 14

69    Maning

Palmetier

Ostranders

64  to Wappings C.

N

to Oswego

L
L  63  M

to Wappings Creek

L  62

L
L  L
L  L
61

K    Symeo's  I

R  68  Gen Dubois

Wappings Cr.

Q

Van D. Water  67

to Oswego

P
66  Filkin

Le Roy

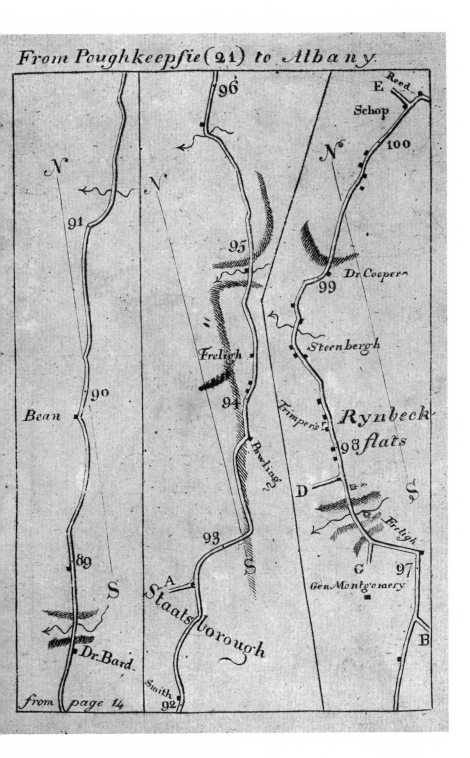

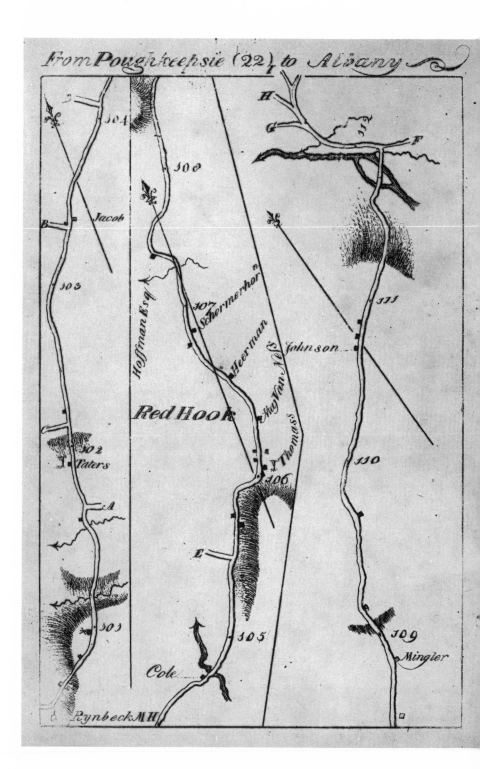

From Poughkeepsie (22) to Albany

142

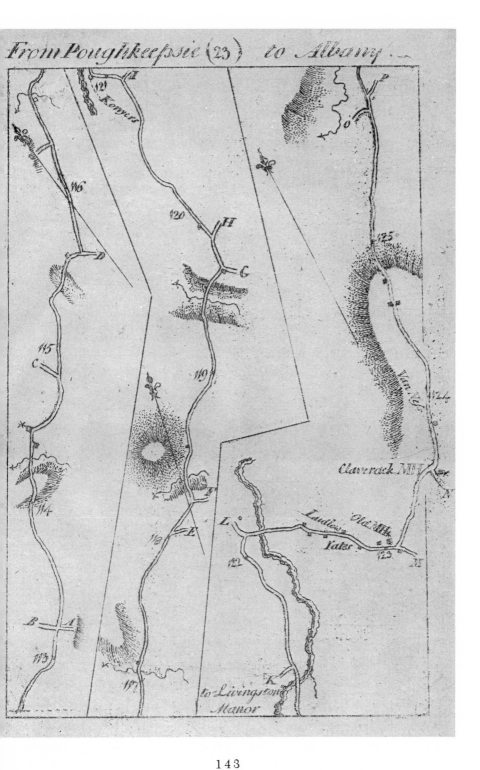

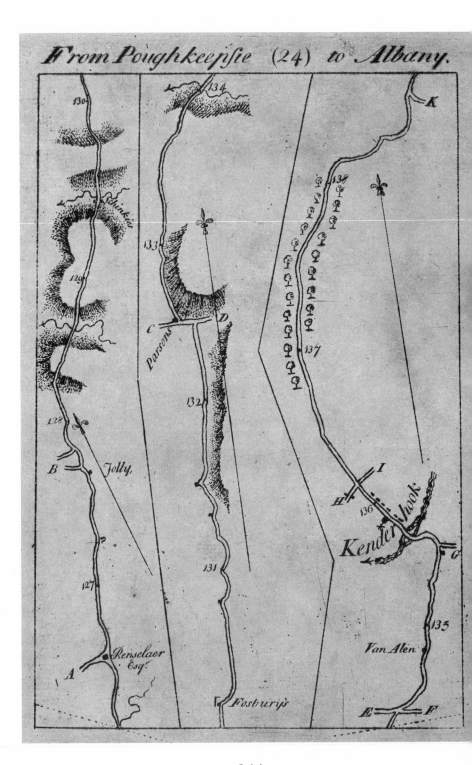

From Poughkeepsie (25) to Albany.

143
Miller
147
142
151
146
Valkenburgh
Lodewick
to Barrington
150
141
145
140
149
144
A
Murder's Creek
139

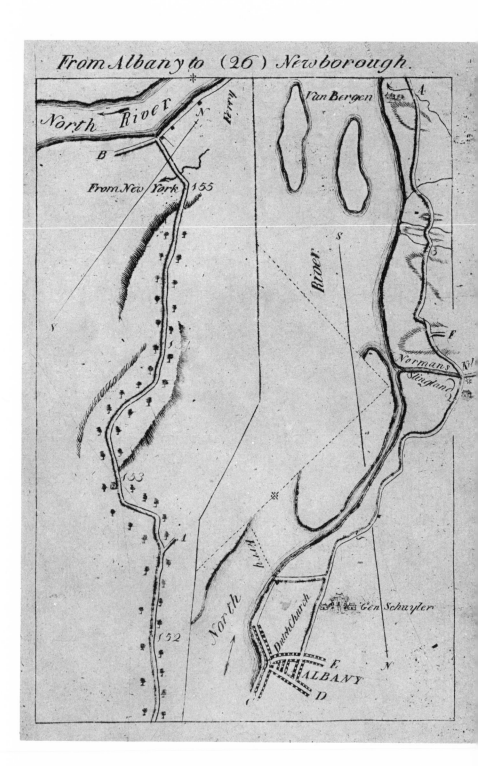

From Albany to (26) Newborough.

North River

Van Bergen

B

From New York 155

Ferry

River

Normans Kil

Slingland

153

A

152

North

Dutch church

Gen Schuyler

ALBANY

E

D

C

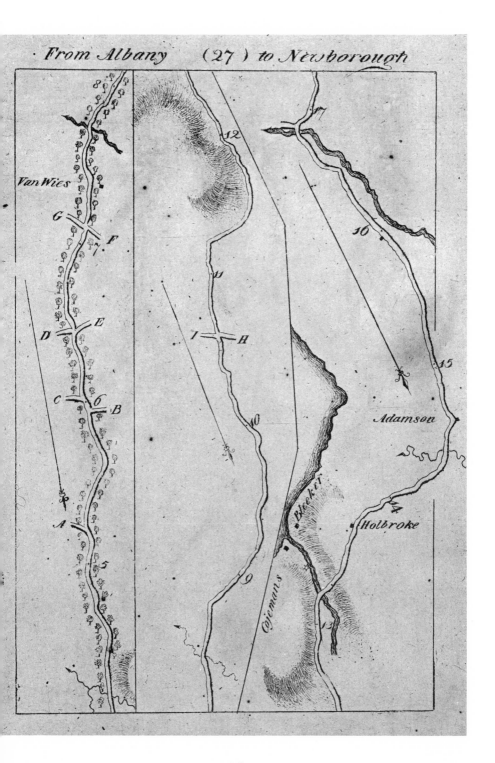

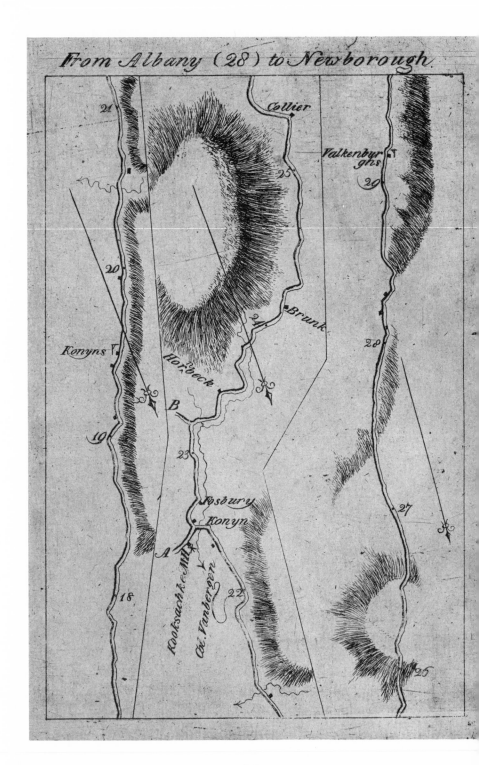

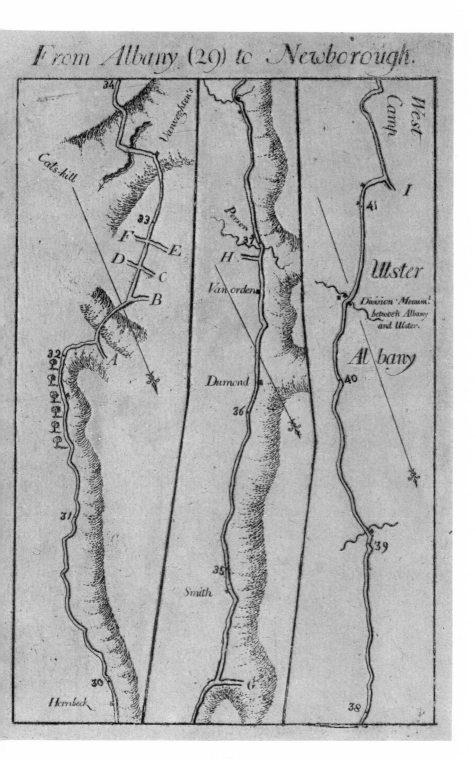

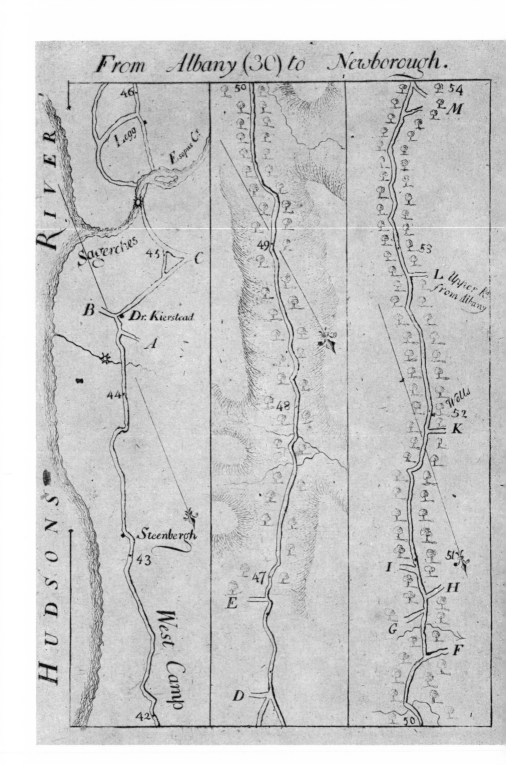

150

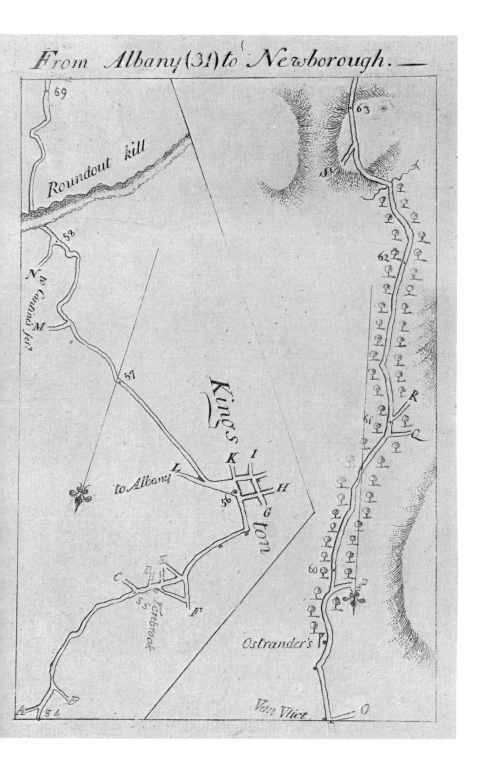

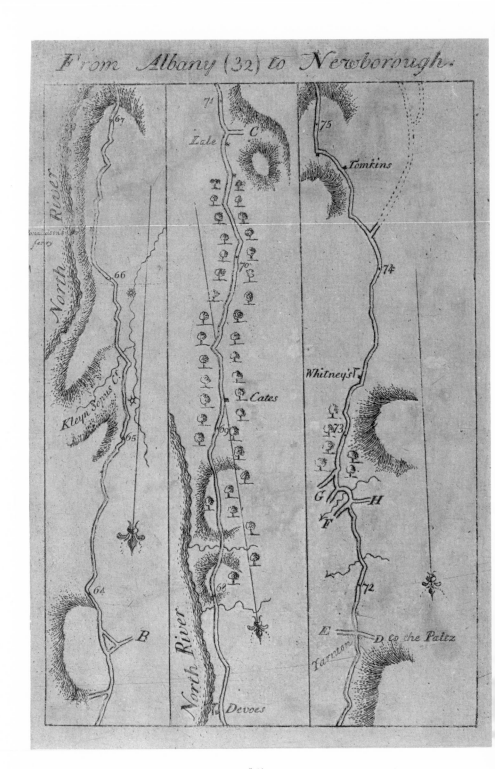

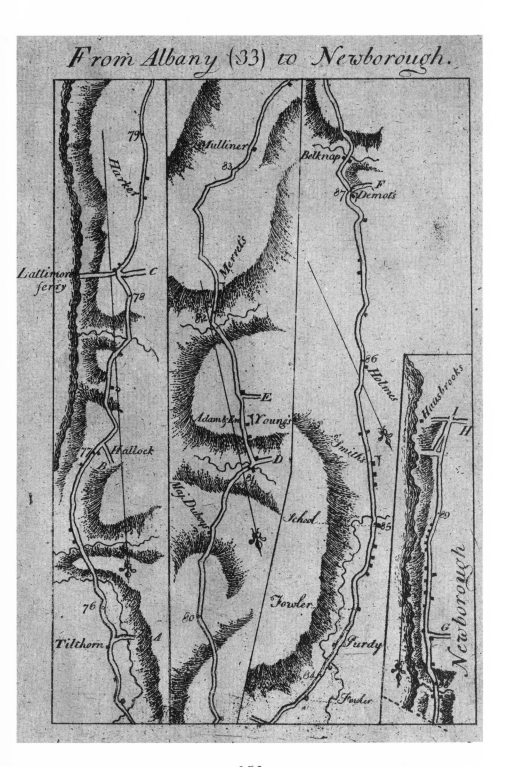

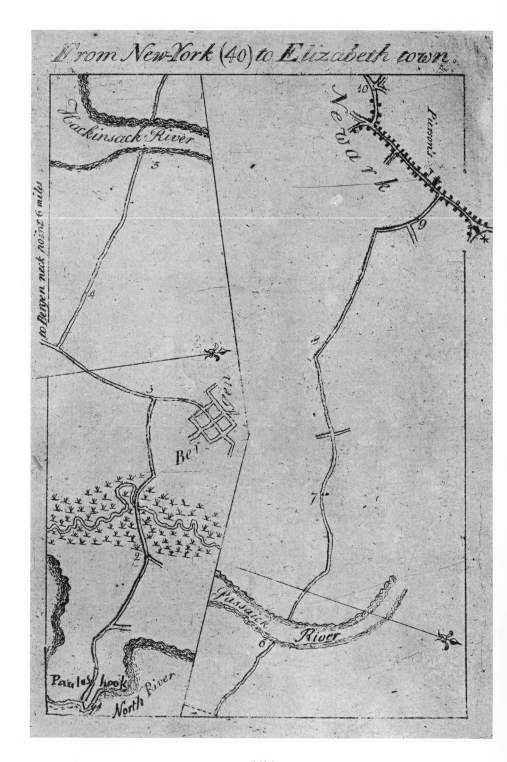

From New-York (40) to Elizabeth town.

Hackinsack River

Newark

Pissmi

to Bergen next point 6 miles

10

9

5

4

3

Be r gen

8

North River

Paulus hook

Pussaick River

7

6

2

154

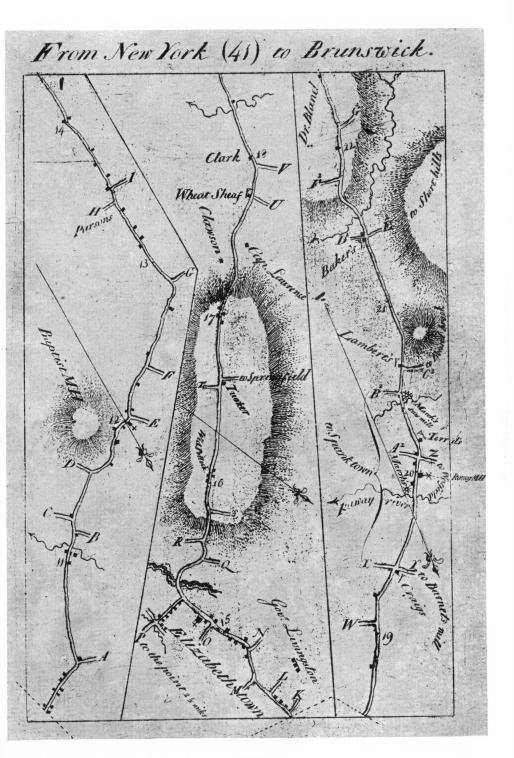

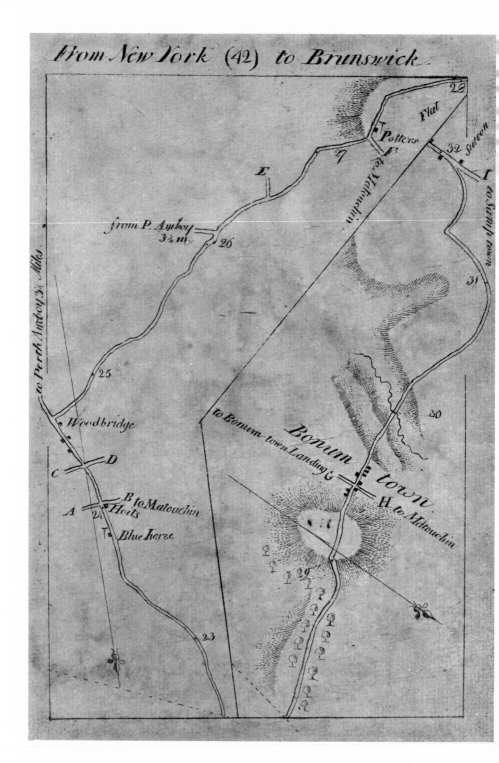

From New York (42) to Brunswick

22

Flat

Potters
F

27

32 Suron

E

to Sample town

from P. Amboy
3¾ m
26

to Middletin

31

to Perch Amboy 3¾ Miles

25

30

Woodbridge

to Bonum town Landing

Bonum town

D
C

G

B to Matouchin
Hoits
A 24

H. to Matouchin

Blue horse

29

23

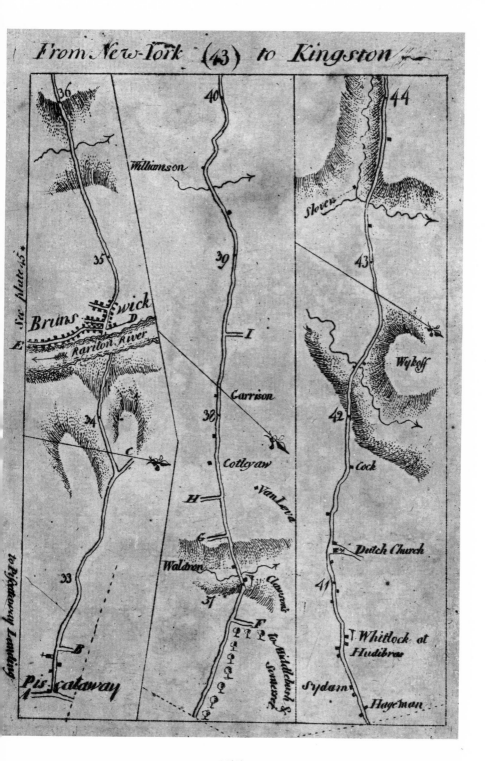

From New-York (43) to Kingston

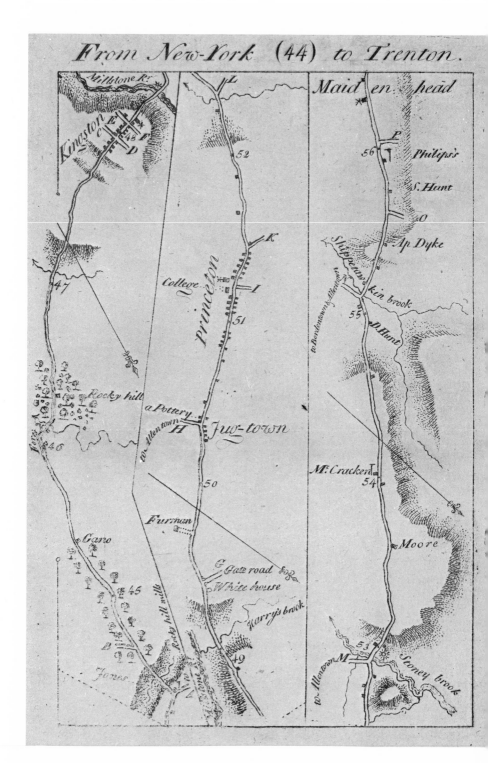

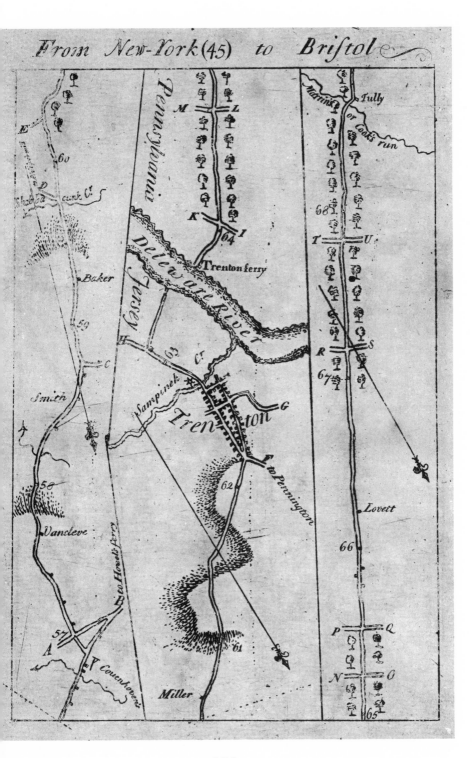

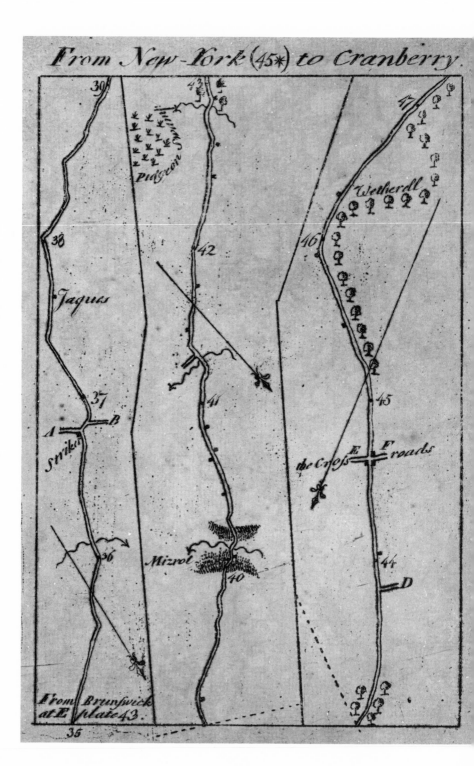

*From New-York (45✱) to Cranberry.*

39

43

Pidgeon Swamp

42

38

Jaques

Wetherell

46

37
A  B
Striker

41

45

the Cross E. F. roads

36

Mizrol

40

44

D

From Brunswick
at E plate 43.

35

160

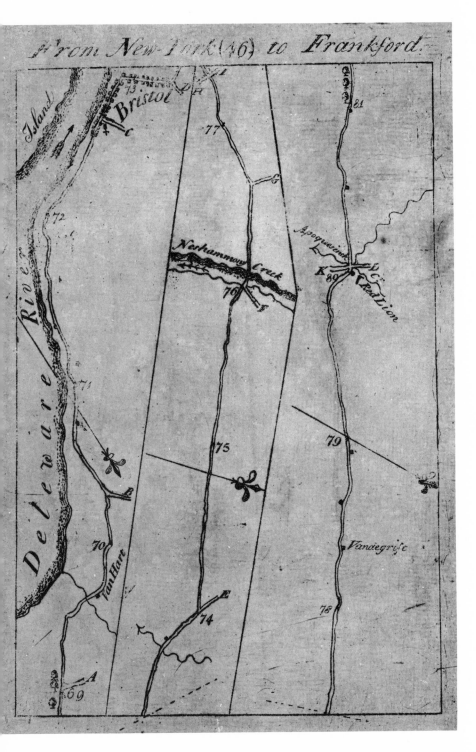

From New-York (46) to Frankford.

161

51

H 55 I
School

Shrewsbury Rd

59

50 E

54

58

Cran D berry

C

Dto Princeton

49

G 53

Alleckson at
Crooked billet

Cat tail
57

Wards
Rocky
town
Hights brook

Sampinck brook

48

F Hight
52

56

Story

A

From New York (47) to Philadelphia.

85

Wheat Sheaf

84

89

88

Frankford Cr.

Holmes's Frankford

C
D
B

H E87 G

F

82

A

86

E

Philadelphia

Market Street

92 Cho qui no quik
Barrack

Cohocs

K
Smick

91

I

90

163

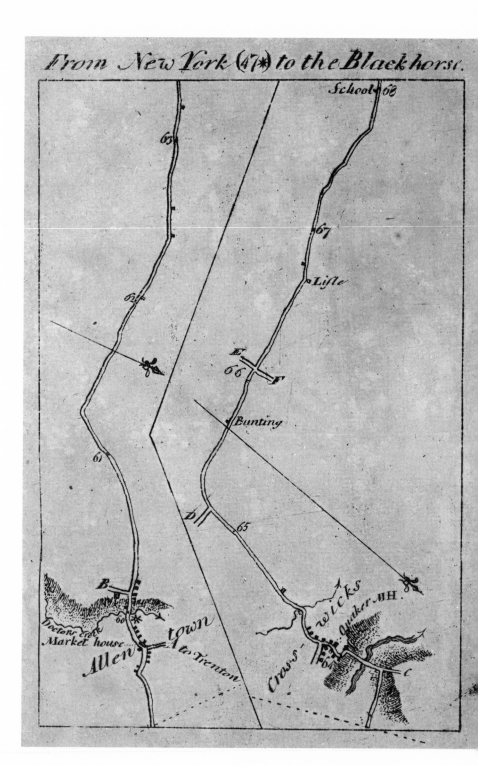

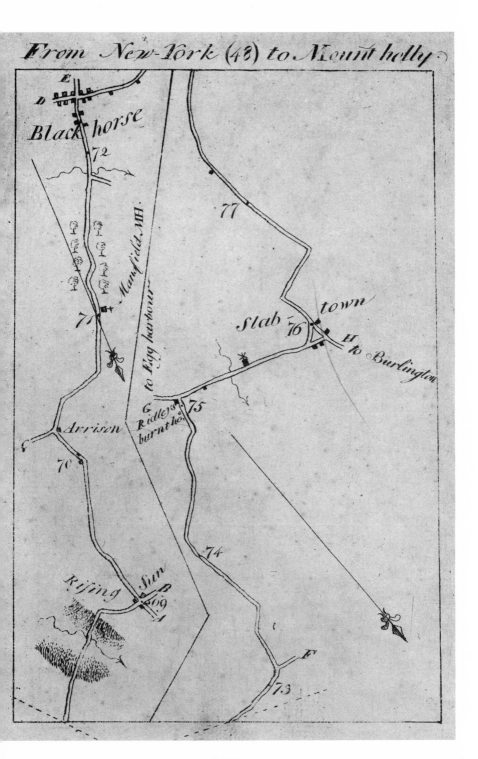

Black horse

E
D

72

Mansfield MH.

to Egg harbour

71

77

Slab 76 town

H to Burlington

G Ridley's 75
burnt ho.

Arrison

70

74

Rising Sun
B
69
A

F

73

165

From New-York (49) to Philadelphia.

Ancocas waters

86

P

O

T

Moors town

90

N

85

T. McCalley's
Inglis

G

82

E
F
A
D
North Branch
of Ancocas
Tide rises to the road
C

Mount Holly town

80

Moors town

8

89

M

Holly

Mount

A

B

K

4

L

R

79

H

I

88

Q

School

South branch of Ancocas

Lippingwill

23
Tide goes 3 or 4 mile higher

87

78

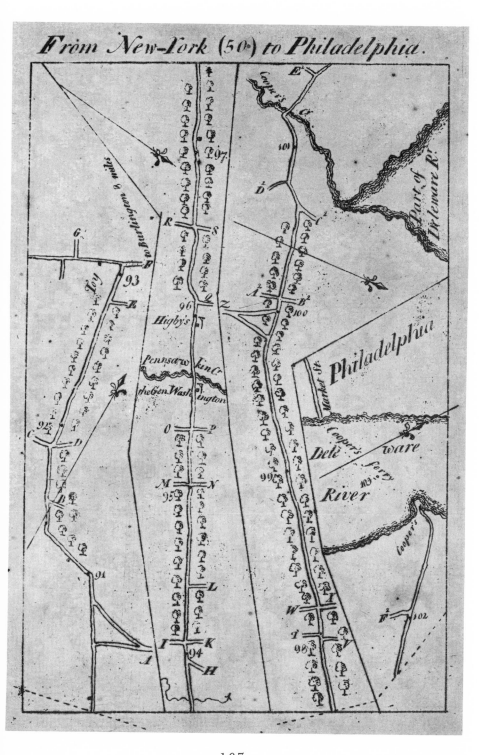

From New-York (50) to Philadelphia.

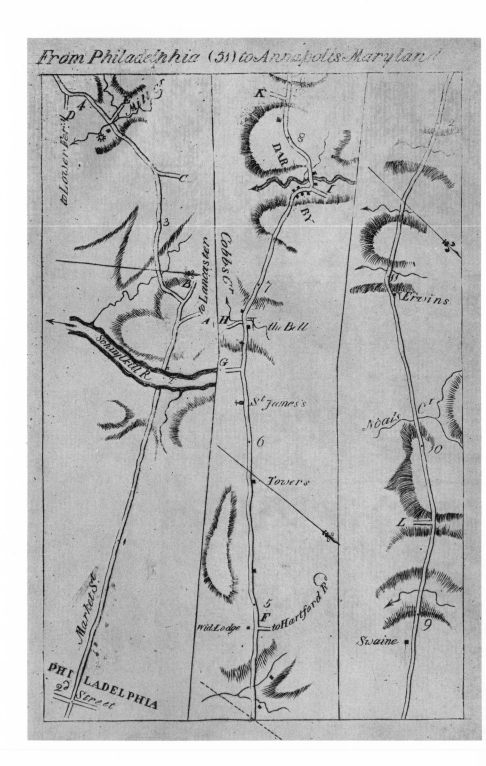

From Philadelphia (51) to Annapolis Maryland

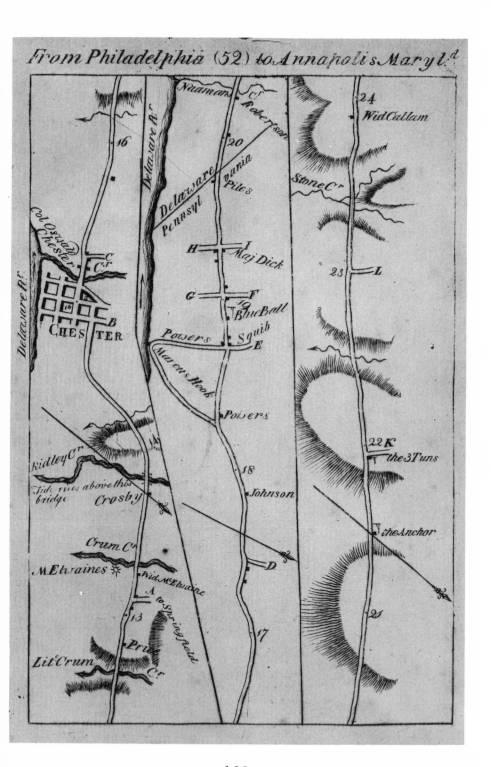

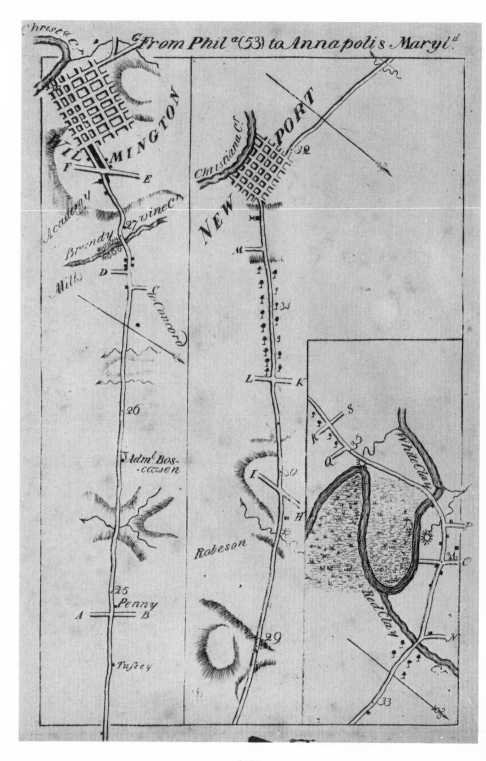

From Phil.ᵃ (53) to Annapolis Maryl.ᵈ

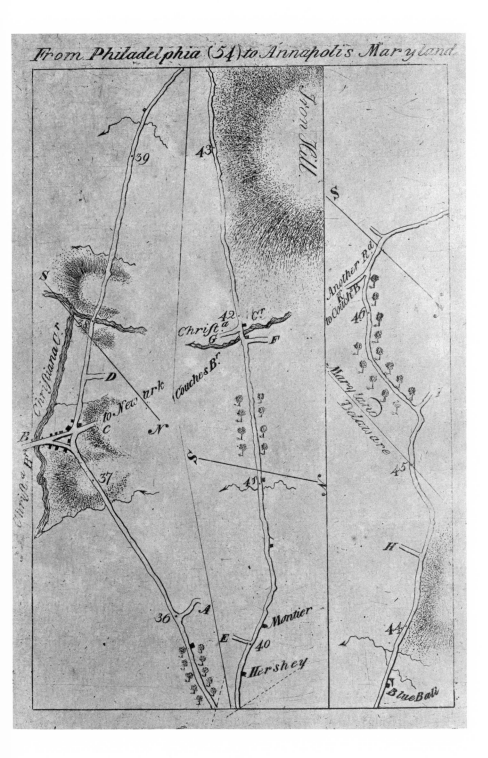

From Philadelphia (54) to Annapolis Maryland

# From Philadelphia (55) to Annapolis Maryl.ᵈ

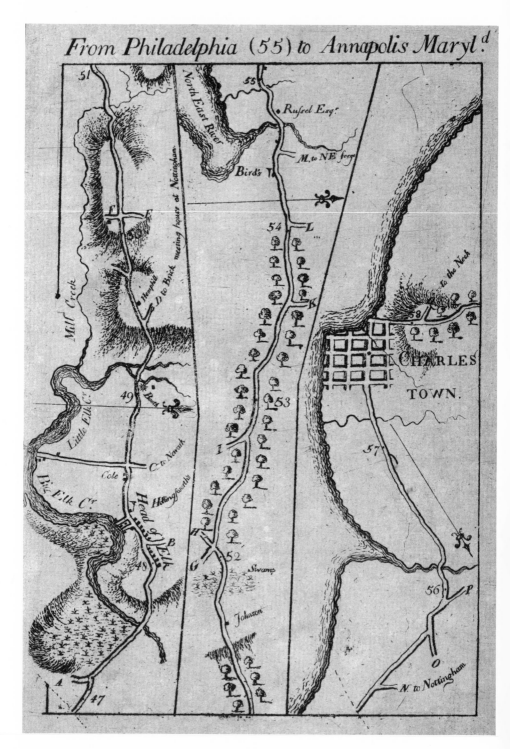

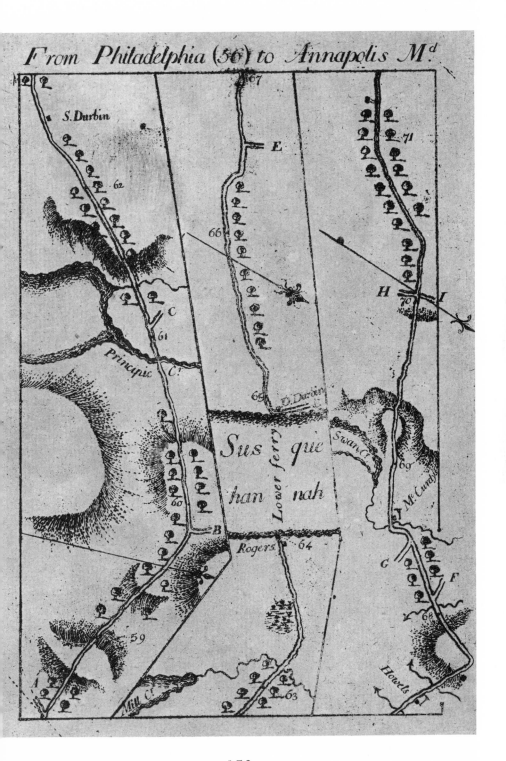

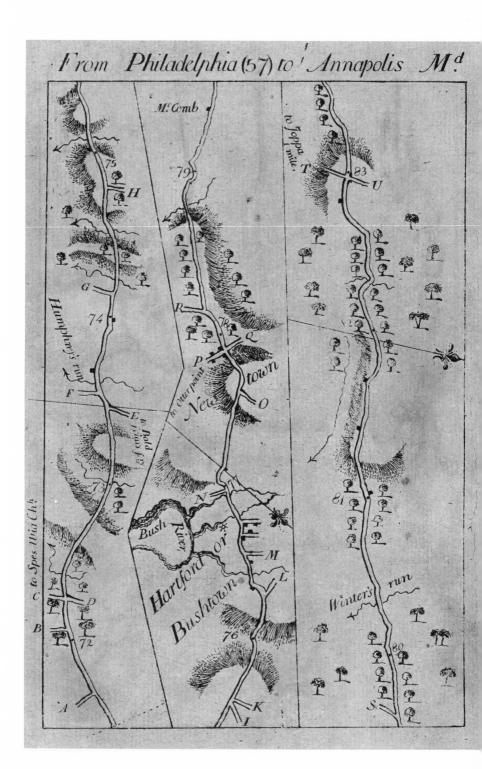

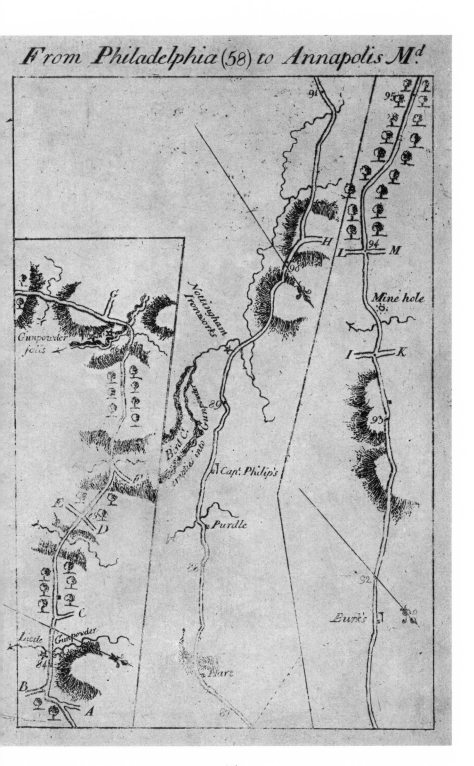

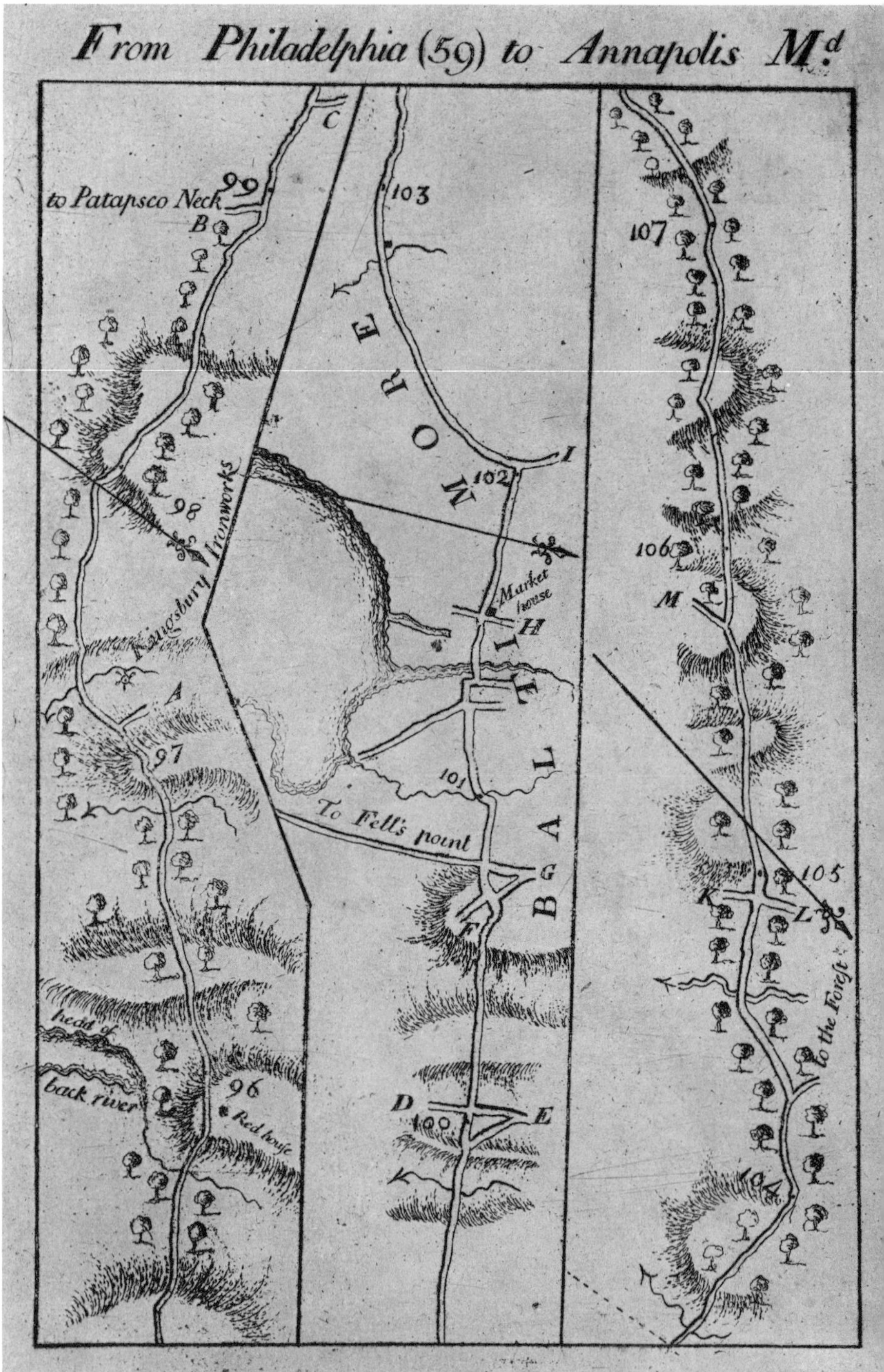

C

to Patapsco Neck
99
B
103

MOREN

98
I
102
Kingsbury Ironworks
Market house
H

A
97
BALTI

To Fell's point
101
G

head of
back river
96
Red house
D 100 E

107

106
M

105
K L

to the Forest

104

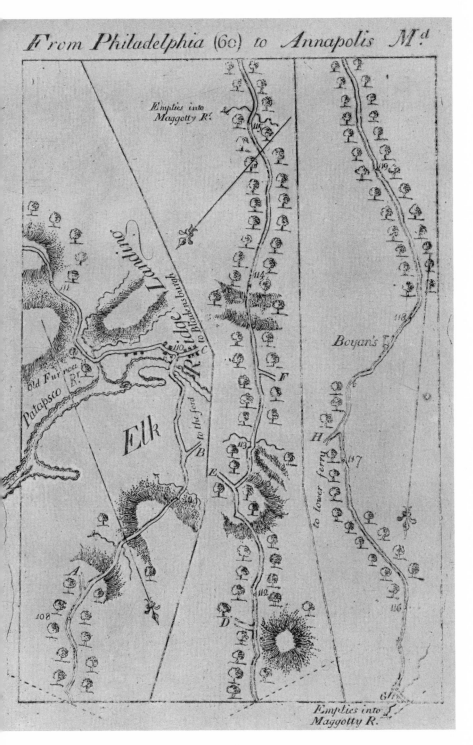

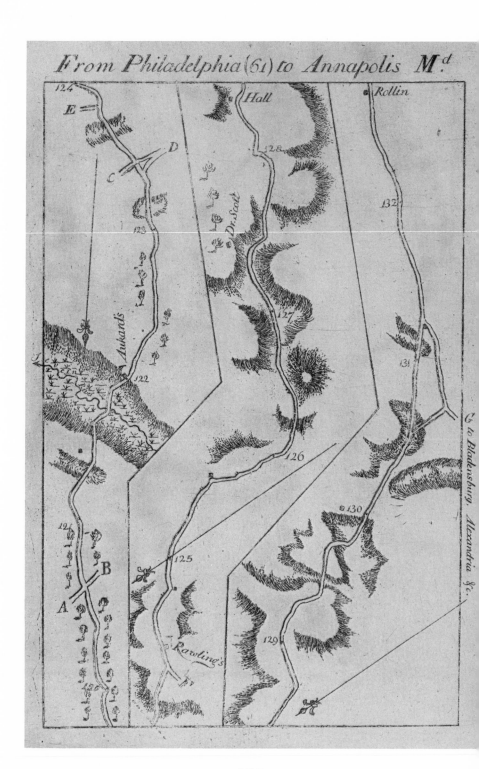

## From Annapolis (62) to Bladensburg.

North run
Hog-neck
run
D
Mußer
6
Head of Broad Creek
5
134
ANNA POLIS
Wetherington's
4
B
A
133
C
From G Plate 61

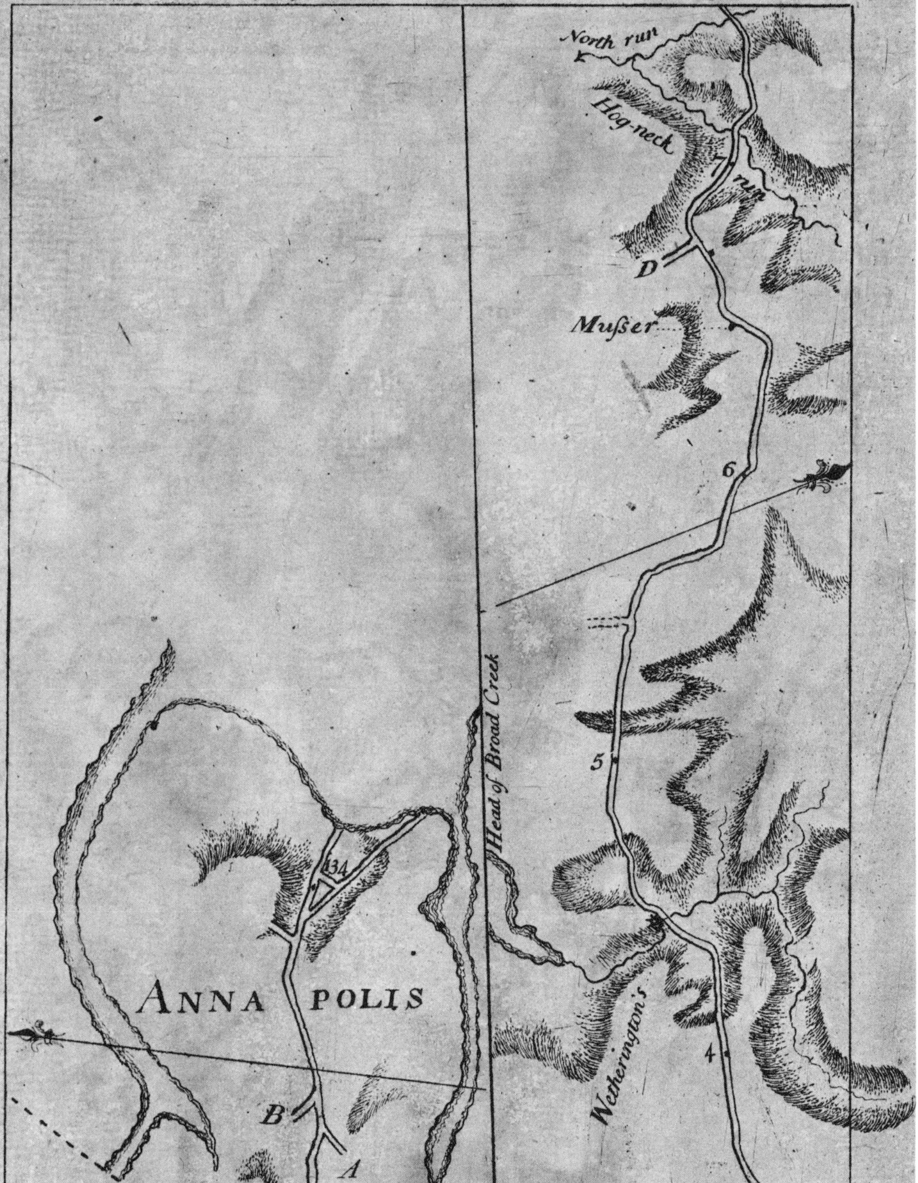

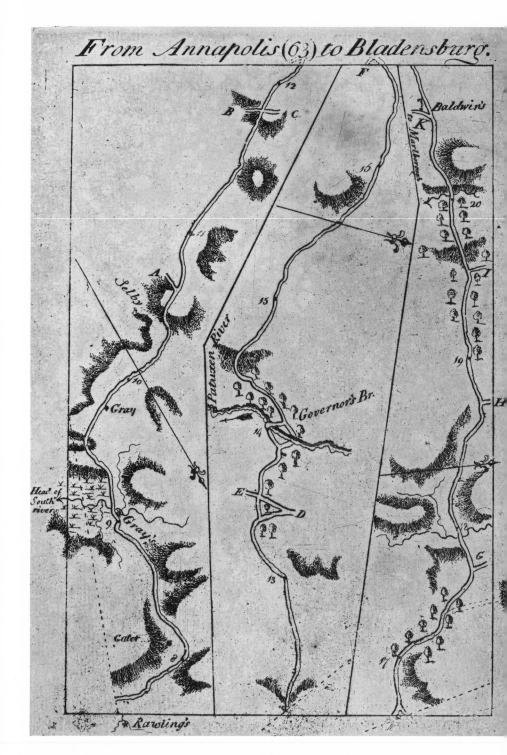

From Annapolis (63) to Bladensburg.

From Annapolis (64) to Alexandria.

From Annapolis (65) to Alexandria.

G    H
58
Pohick    run
Boggs
N. to Parry's ferry
M
to Newgate
57    L
K    Pohick Church
49
Gen. Washington's Land
53
F
to Pohick Warehouse
52
56    Cr.
Accohick
48
E
to Loudon County
D    C
Mr. Allison
47    B
51
A
I    55
Old Road
Delany Esq.
46
54
50

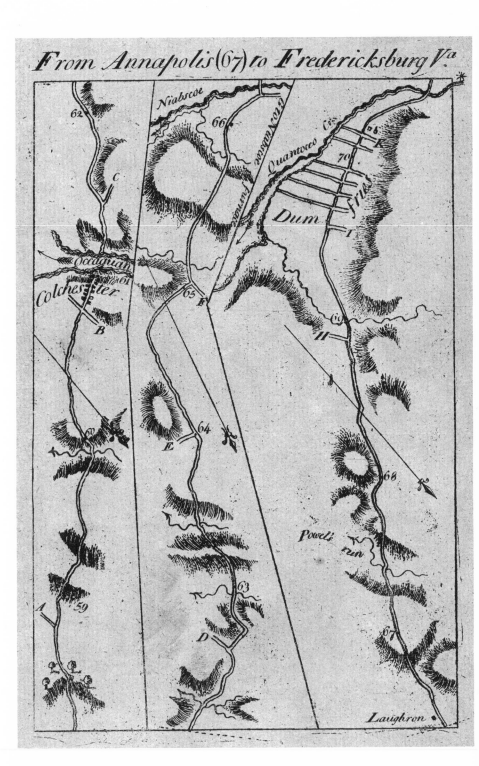

From Annapolis (67) to Fredericksburg V.ᵃ

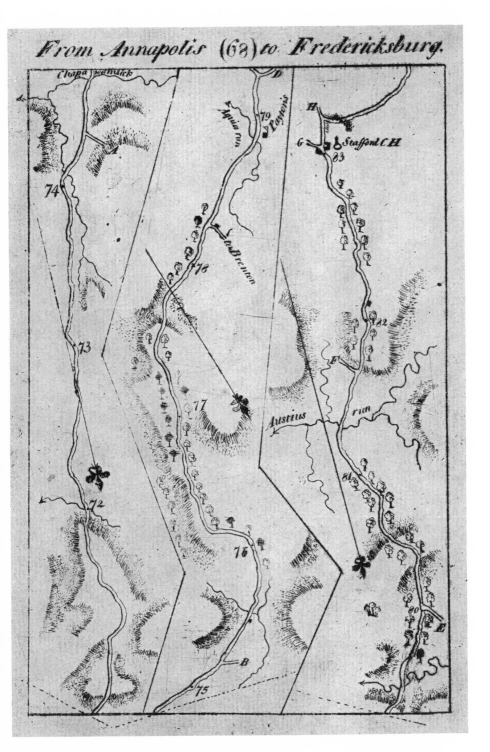

From Annapolis (69) to Todd's Ordinary.

186

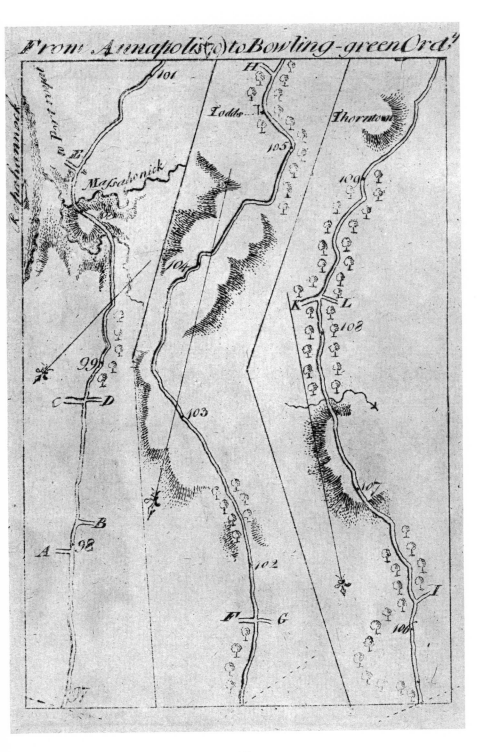

From Annapolis(o) to Bowling-green Ord.ᵈ

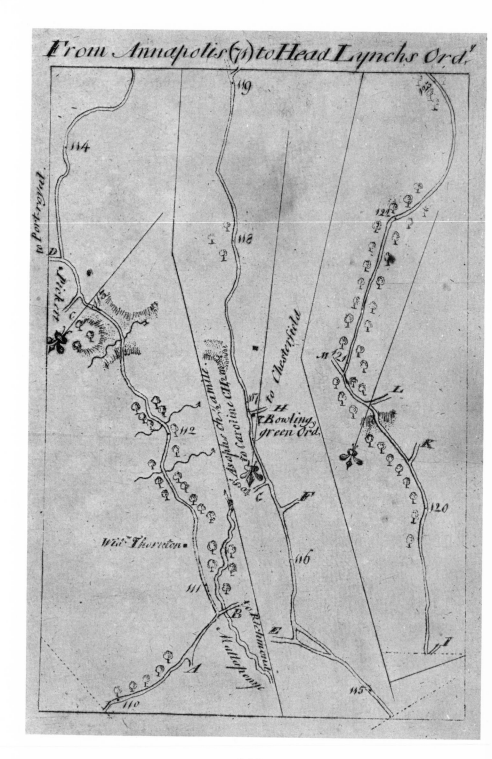

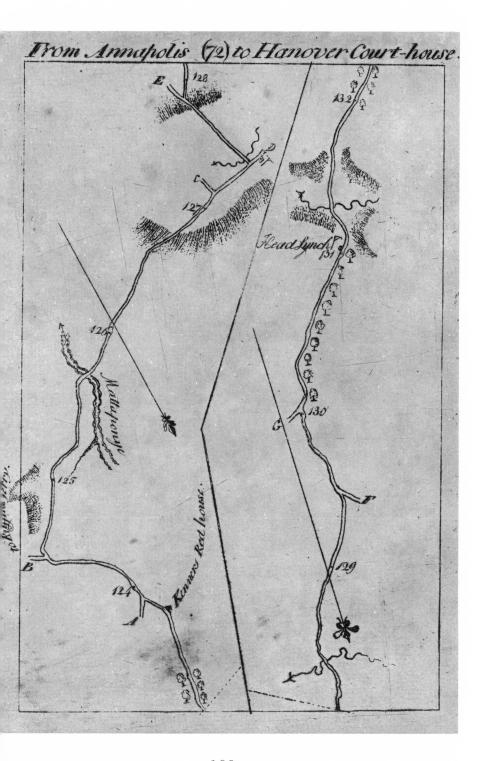

From Annapolis (72) to Hanover Court-house.

189

From Annapolis (73) to Hanover & Newcastle.

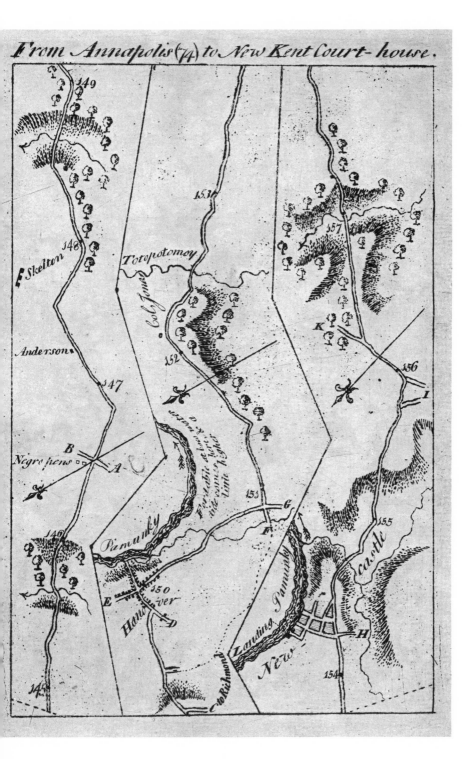

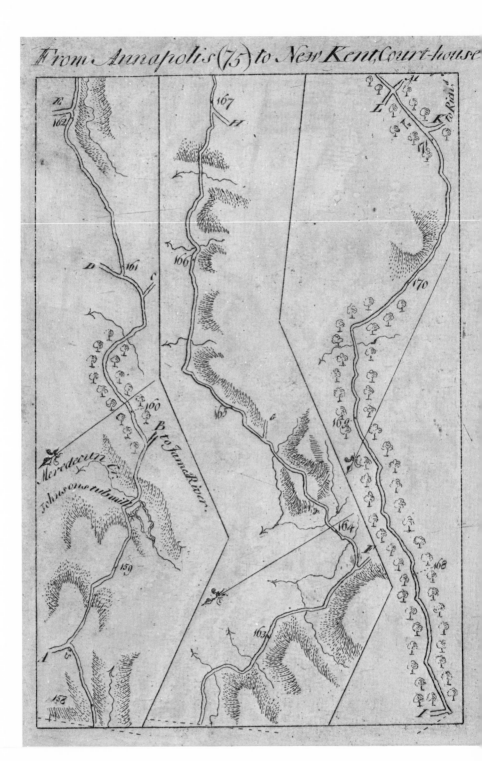

192

# From Annapolis (76) to Williamsburgh.

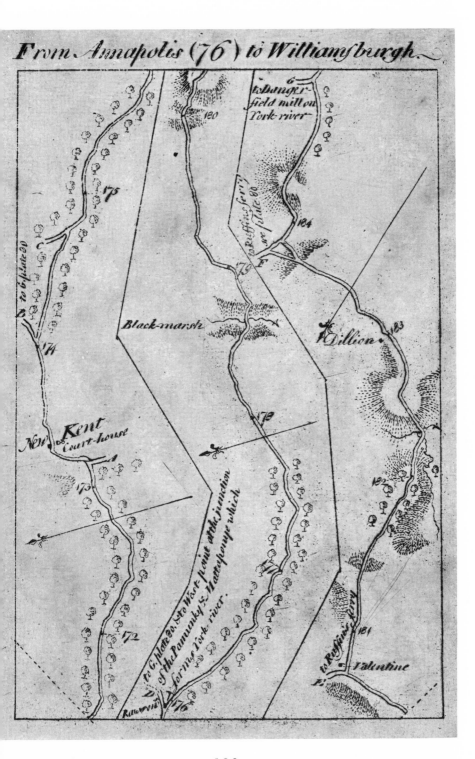

193

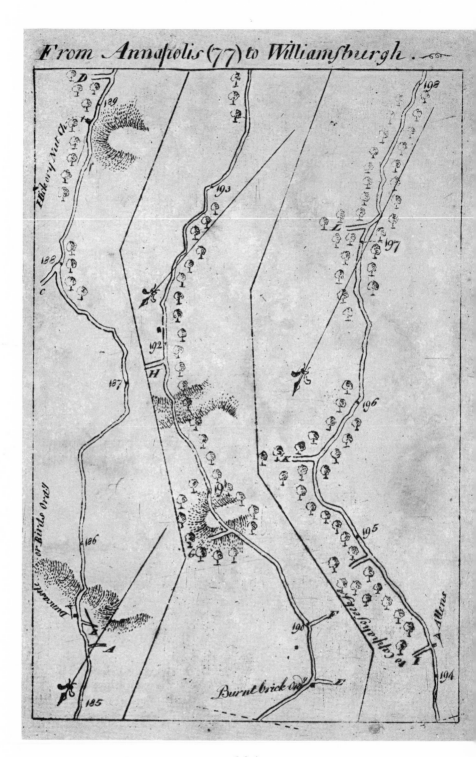

From Annapolis (77) to Williamsburgh.

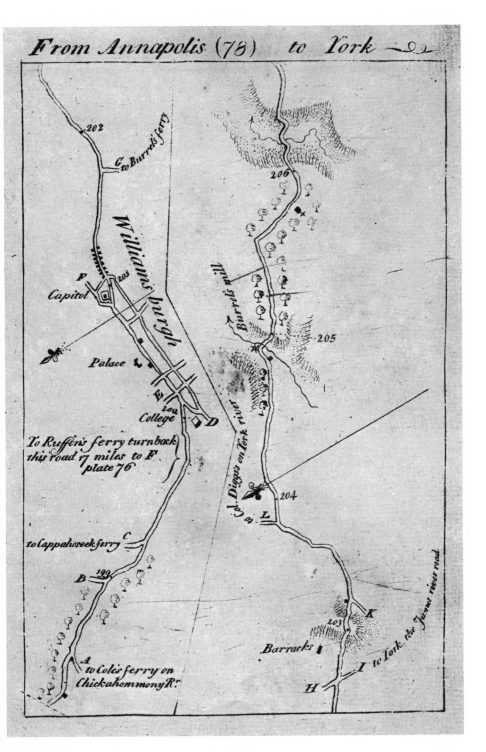

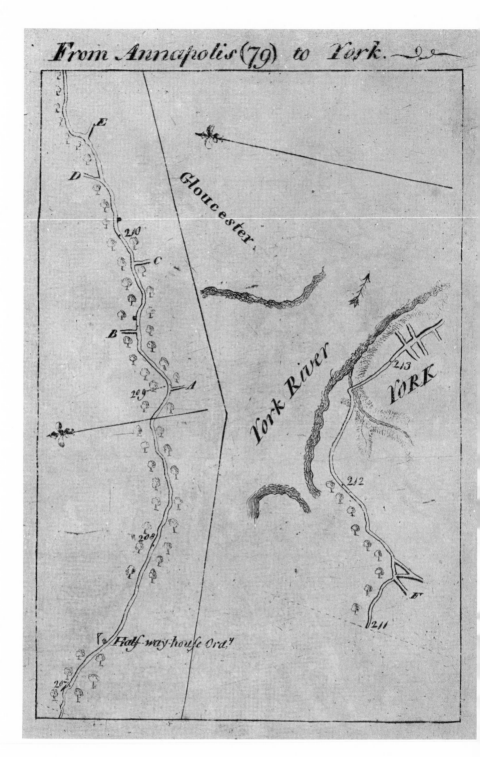

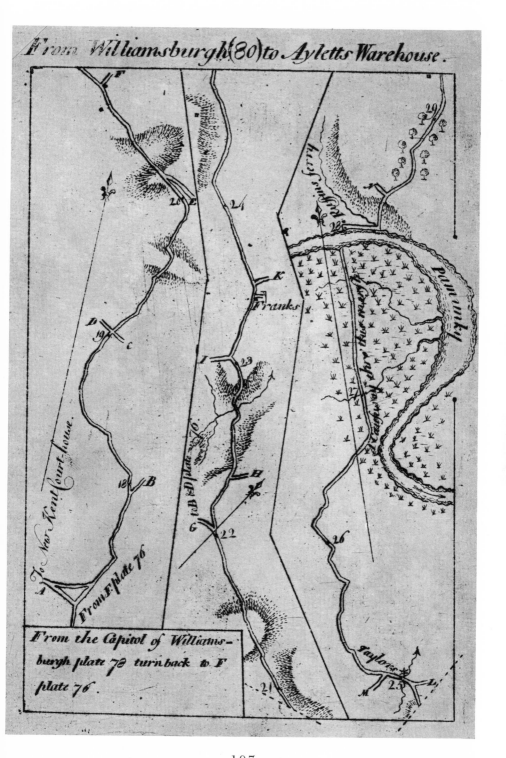

From Williamsburgh (80) to Ayletts Warehouse.

From the Capitol of Williamsburgh plate 78 turn back to F
plate 76.

197

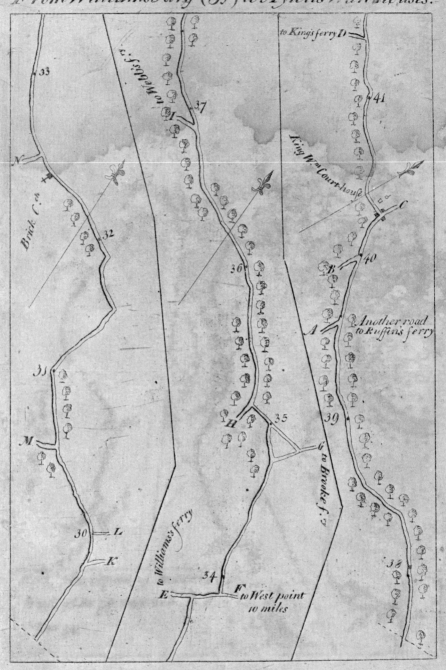

From Williamsburg (82) to Sneed's Ordinary.

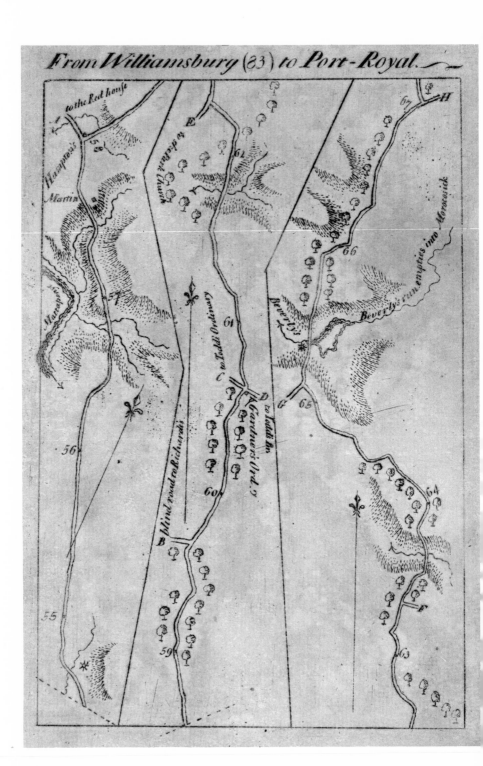

# From Williamsburg (83) to Port-Royal.

# From Williamsburg (84) to Port-royal.

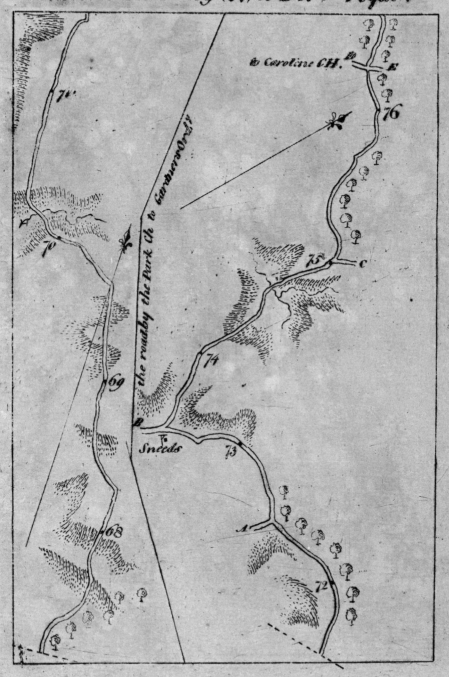

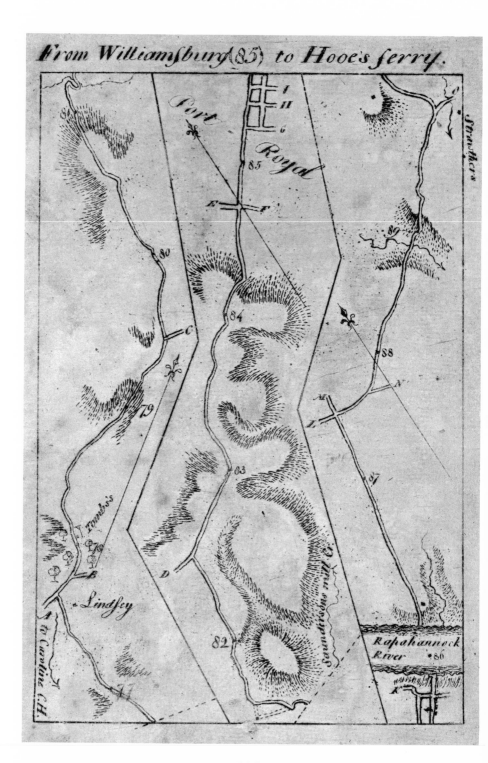

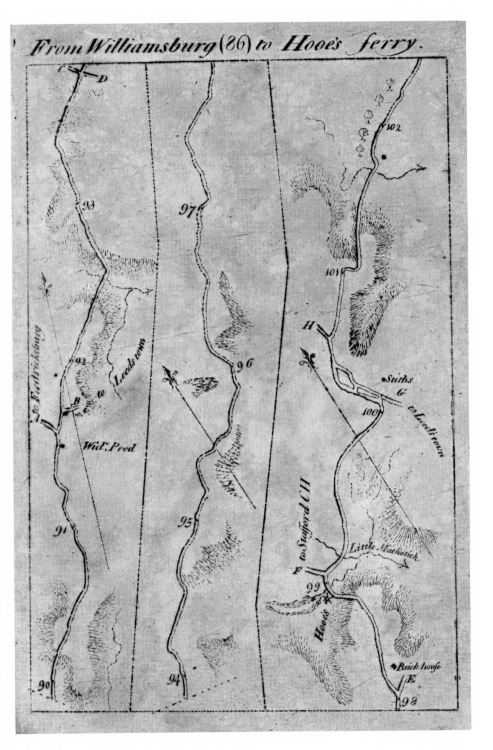

*Alphabetical Index*
*Classified Index*
*Index to Part One*

# Alphabetical Index to
## Colles' *Survey of the Roads of the United States of America*

| Name | Plate No. | Name | Plate No. |
|------|-----------|------|-----------|
| Abrams | 2 | Baker | 45 |
| Acher | 9 | Baker's, tavern | 41 |
| Adam & Eve | 33 | Baldwin's, tavern | 63 |
| Adamson | 27 | Baldwin's, Col., tavern | 16 |
| Adamson's, tavern | 1 | Baptist Meeting House | 41 |
| Adams's, grist mill | 65 | Bard, Dr. | 21 |
| Addington | 3 | Barker | 3 |
| Albany | 26 | Barrack (Philadelphia) | 47 |
| Alben | 16 | Barracks (near Williamsburgh) | 78 |
| Alexandria, Va. | 65 | Barret | 10 |
| Allen's, tavern | 77 | Barton | 3 |
| Allentown, N. J. | 47* | Barton | 9 |
| Alleckson at Crooked | | Bate | 4 |
| billet, tavern | 46* | Bayrum | 3 |
| The Anchor, tavern | 52 | Beach | 16 |
| Ancocas River, North Branch | 49 | Bean | 21 |
| Ancocas River, South Branch | 49 | Beech's, tavern | 15 |
| Ancocas Waters | 49 | Beekman | 1 |
| Anderson | 74 | Belknap | 33 |
| Annapolis, Md. | 62 | The Bell, tavern | 51 |
| Annen | 12 | Belle air | 63 |
| Ap Dyke | 44 | Benedict | 5 |
| Apoquesinck Creek | 46 | Bennet | 5 |
| Aquia Run | 68 | Bennet's, tavern | 15 |
| Archer's, tavern | 8 | Bergen, N. J. | 40 |
| Arrison | 48 | Betts | 2 |
| Attwood | 1 | Betts | 4 |
| Aukard's, tavern | 61 | Betts', tavern | 5 |
| Austius Run | 68 | Beverly's Run | 83 |
| Aylett's, grist mill | 82 | Big Elk Creek | 55 |
| Aylett's Warehouses | 82 | Bird Creek | 58 |
| | | Bird's, tavern | 55 |
| Bailey (2) | 3 | | |

| Name | Plate No. | Name | Plate No. |
|------|-----------|------|-----------|
| Birds Ordinary | | Boyan's, tavern | 60 |
| see Duncastle Ordinary | | Brandywine Creek | 53 |
| Birdsall's, tavern | 10 | Brevoort | 1 |
| Blackhorse, N. J. | 48 | Brick Church (Epis.) | 81 |
| Blackman, tavern | 16 | Brick House | 86 |
| Black-marsh Creek | 76 | Briggs | 2 |
| Blacksmith shop | | Bristol, N. J. | 46 |
| (Near Benedict) | 5 | Broad Creek | 62 |
| Blacksmith shop | | Bronner | 9 |
| (Near Mason) | 10 | Brook's, tavern | 15 |
| Blacksmith shop | | Brower | 13 |
| (Near Noxon) | 19 | Brown | 8 |
| Blacksmith shop | | Brownell's, tavern | 18 |
| (N. of Palmar) | 3 | Brunk | 28 |
| Blacksmith shop | | Brunks [Bronx] River | 2 |
| (W. of Rye) | 3 | Brunswick, N.J. | 43 |
| Blacksmith shop | | Brush | 3 |
| (Near Walker) | 15 | Buchanon | 1 |
| Blackwell | 16 | Buchanon | 69 |
| Bladensburgh, Md. | 64 | Budd (2) | 11 |
| Bland, Dr. | 41 | Budd, Col. | 3 |
| Bleeker | 27 | Bunting | 47 |
| Bloomer | 12 | Burk's, tavern | 58 |
| Blue Ball, tavern | 52 | Burnt brick Ordinary, tavern | 77 |
| Blue Bull, tavern | 54 | Burnt Ordinary | 82 |
| Blue Horse, tavern | 42 | Burr (2) | 16 |
| Bonumtown, N. J. | 42 | Burrels | 7 |
| Booth | 5 | Burrel's mill | 78 |
| Booth | 15 | Burrels, tavern | 5 |
| Booth, grist mill | 55 | Burying ground | |
| Booth, Capt. | 15 | (Near Ripley's) | 5 |
| Boring Mill | | Bush | 3 |
| (Near Fredericksburgh) | 69 | Bush | 4 |
| Borrum's, tavern | 14 | Bushtown | |
| Boscawen, Adm., tavern | 53 | see Hartford, Md. | |
| Bossing | 1 | Bye Road | 2 |
| Botsford | 16 | | |
| Boughton | 17 | Callam, Wid. | 52 |
| Boutten | 4 | Camp | 16 |
| Bowling Green | | Cates | 32 |
| Ordinary (tavern) | 71 | Catskill | 29 |
| Bownes, mill | 3 | Chandler's, Gen., tavern | 16 |

# ALPHABETICAL INDEX

| Name | Plate No. | Name | Plate No. |
|---|---|---|---|
| Chapawansick River | 68 | Crager | 1 |
| Charlestown, Md. | 55 | Craig's | 41 |
| Chatherton | 10 | Cranberry, N.J. | 46* |
| Chester, Pa. | 52 | Crawford's, tavern | 2 |
| Chester Creek | 52 | Crofts | 11 |
| Cho-que-no-quok Creek | 47 | Cronk | 10 |
| Christiana Creek | 53 & 54 | Crooks | 14 |
| Church | 5 | Crosby | 52 |
| Clark | 41 | Crossroads, The | 45* |
| Clark, Cap., tavern | 17 | Crosswicks, N.J. | 47* |
| Claverack Meeting House | 23 | Croton River | 9, 17, 18 |
| Clawson | 41 | Crum Creek | 52 |
| Clawson's, tavern | 43 | Crum Elbows's Creek | 14 |
| Clerk | 10 | Curtis | 15 |
| Clifts Store | 5 | | |
| Clock | 4 | Dale | 32 |
| Cobb's Creek | 51 | Danbury, Conn. | 17 |
| Cock | 43 | Darby, Pa. | 51 |
| Coe | 15 | Davenport | 1 |
| Cohocksinck Creek | 47 | Davis | 9 |
| Cojemans | 27 | Days, tavern | 1 |
| Colchester, Va. | 67 | Dayton | 4 |
| Cole | 22 | Deal & Guion | 3 |
| Collier | 28 | Deans, tavern | 1 |
| Conklin | 10 | Delancy | 1 |
| Continental Village, N.Y. | 11 | Delaware River | 45, 46, 50, 52 |
| Cooks, tavern | 18 | Delezenne, tavern | 9 |
| Cook's Run | | Delong's, tavern | 19 |
|   *see* Martin's Run | | Demot's, tavern | 33 |
| Cooper, Dr. | 21 | Dennis's, grist mill | 19 |
| Coopers, tavern, | | Dennis's, tavern | 19 |
|   blacksmith shop | 12 | DePue | 11 |
| Cooper's Creek | 50 | Devoe's, tavern | 32 |
| Cooper's Ferry | 50 | Dick, Maj. | 52 |
| Cortlandt, grist mills | 8 | Dijckman | 10 |
| Cortlandt, Lt. Gov. | 11 | Dillion | 76 |
| Cotleyaw | 43 | Division Monument | |
| Couch | 5 |   (Between Albany & | |
| Couches Bridge | 54 |   Ulster Counties) | 29 |
| Couenhoven's, tavern | 45 | Dobbs's Ferry, N.Y. | 8 |
| Covenhoven | 9 | Doctor's Creek | 47* |
| Covenhoven, tavern | 9 | Donaldson's Ferry | 32 |

| Name | Plate No. | Name | Plate No. |
|------|------|------|------|
| Dorland, blacksmith shop | 19 | Fraer's, tavern | 13 |
| Drake's, tavern | 9 | Frankford, N.J. | 47 |
| Drake's, Col., mill | 9 | Frankford, creek | 47 |
| Dumfries, Va. | 67 | Frank's, tavern | 80 |
| Dumond | 29 | Fredericksburgh, Va. | 69 |
| Duncastle *or* Bird's | | Freligh | 21 |
| Ordinary (tavern) | 77 | Freligh, mill | 21 |
| Dunkin | 3 | Frenck's, tavern | 15 |
| Durbin, D. | 56 | Frost | 13 |
| Durbin, S. | 56 | Fulling Mill | |
| Duryee | 1 | (Near Hunt's) | 8 |
| Dusenbury's, tavern | 8, 11 | | |
| Dutch Church (Albany) | 26 | Gaine | 1 |
| Dutch Church (Presb.) | 43 | Gano | 44 |
| Dutchess County, N.Y. | 17 | Gardner's Ordinary | |
| | | (tavern) | 83 |
| East Chester, N.Y. | 2 | Garison | 11 |
| Elizabethtown, N.J. | 41 | Garrison | 43 |
| Elk Ridge Landing, Md. | 60 | Gates | 63 |
| Ellis | 1 | Gen. Washington, The, tavern | 50 |
| Englehart | 1 | Georgetown, Md. | 65 |
| Episcopal Church | | Gidney | 3 |
| (Near Philips's) | 8 | Gidney, blacksmith shop | 3 |
| Erwins, tavern | 51 | Gloucester, Va. | 79 |
| Esopus Creek | 30 | Goelchins | 10 |
| | | Governor's Bridge | 63 |
| Fairfield, Conn. | 6 | Gray | 63 |
| Falmouth, Va. | 69 | Gray's, grist mill | 63 |
| Fansher | 4 | Great Rock | 3 |
| Federal Hall (New York City) | 1 | Grierson's, tavern | 1 |
| Filkin | 20 | Grifins | 10 |
| Fish Kill, N.Y. | 12 | Grist mill | |
| Flandreau, blacksmith shop | 3 | (Near New York State line) | 17 |
| Forsyth | 11 | Grist mill (Near Capt. Booth) | 15 |
| Ft. Washington, N.Y. | 1 | Grist mill (Near Boutten) | 4 |
| Fort's, tavern | 44 | Guion | 2, 3 |
| Fosburg's, tavern | 24 | Guion, Esq. | 2 |
| Fosbury | 28 | Gunpowder Falls | 58 |
| Fowler | 2 | | |
| Fowler (2) | 33 | Hackinsack River | 40 |
| Fraer | 13 | Hageman | 43 |
| Fraer, Col. | 13 | Haight | 10 |

# ALPHABETICAL INDEX

| Name | Plate No. | Name | Plate No. |
|---|---|---|---|
| Haight, Capt. | 12 | Hog-neck Run | 62 |
| Half-way-house | | Hoits | 42 |
| Ordinary, tavern | 79 | Holbroke | 27 |
| Haley | 6, 16 | Hollingworth's, tavern | 55 |
| Haley's, tavern | 15 | Holmes | 33 |
| Hall | 61 | Holmes's, tavern | 47 |
| Hallock | 33 | Hooe's, grist mill | 86 |
| Halsey's, tavern | 2 | Hopkins, tavern | 18 |
| Hammond | 10 | Horn | 1 |
| Hampton's | 83 | Hornbeck | 28, 29 |
| Hanover, Va. | 74 | Horses Neck, Conn. | 4 |
| Hanover Court House, Va. | 73 | Horton's, tavern | 3 |
| Hardenbrook | 1 | How | 4 |
| Hare | 3 | Howel's, tavern | 56 |
| Harker | 33 | Hoyt | 5 |
| Harpin | 7 | Hubbel | 4, 7 |
| Harris | 14 | Hudsons River | 30 |
| Harry's Brook | 44 | Hugins, tavern | 18 |
| Hart | 58 | Humphreys Run | 57 |
| Hartford *or* | | Hunt, D. | 44 |
| Bushtown, Md. | 57 | Hunt, S. | 44 |
| Hartshorn | 10 | Hunt, mill | 3 |
| Hausbrooks | 33 | Hunter | 9 |
| Haviland, tavern | 3 | Huntingdon, mill | 2 |
| Haws, P., Esq. | 11 | Hunt's, tavern | 8 |
| Haynes | 10 | Hustead | 2, 12 |
| Hays, Col. | 4 | Hyatt's, tavern | 2 |
| Head of Elk, Md. | 55 | | |
| Head Lynch, tavern | 72 | Inglis, grist mill | 49 |
| Heddy | 3 | Iron Hill | 54 |
| Heerman | 22 | | |
| Hemphill | 55 | | |
| Hendrick's & Pool's, tavern | 14 | Jacob | 22 |
| Hershey | 54 | Jaques | 45* |
| Hickory Nut Church (Epis.) | 77 | Jay | 3 |
| Higby's, tavern | 50 | Jenning | 6 |
| Hight | 46* | Johnson | 22, 52, 55 |
| Hightstown, N.J. | 46* | Johnson's tub mill | 75 |
| Hill | 14 | Jolly | 24 |
| Hinman's, tavern | 15 | Jones | 44 |
| Hoffman, Esq. | 22 | Jones, Col. | 74 |
| Hogeland | 13 | Jug-town, N.J. | 44 |

211

| Name | Plate No. | Name | Plate No. |
|---|---|---|---|
| Kelsey's, tavern | 14 | Little Machotick Creek | 86 |
| Kenderhook, N.Y. | 24 | Livingston | 13 |
| Kenner's Red House, tavern | 72 | Livingston, Gov. | 41 |
| Kierstead, Dr. | 30 | Livingston, P., Esq. | 8 |
| King & Queens County, Va. | 82 | Lockwood | 5 |
| King William County, Va. | 82 | Lodewick | 25 |
| King William Court House, Va. | 81 | Lodge, Widow | 51 |
| Kings Bridge | 2 | Lossing | 19 |
| Kingsbury Iron Works | 59 | Lovett | 45 |
| Kingston, N.Y. | 31, 44 | Ludlow | 23 |
| Kleyn Sopus Creek | 32 | Lyons | 3 |
| Knap | 4, 17 | | |
| Knap's, tavern | 4 | McCalley's, tavern | 49 |
| Knap's Grist & Fulling Mills | 6 | McComb | 57 |
| Konyers | 23 | McCracken's, tavern | 44 |
| Konyn | 28 | McCurdy's, tavern | 56 |
| Konyn's, tavern | 28 | McElwaine, Wid. | 52 |
| Kooksachke Meeting House | 28 | McElwaine's, grist mill | 52 |
| Korbright | 1 | McGowen | 1 |
| | | Maidenhead, N.J. | 44 |
| Lamb's, tavern | 19 | Mansfield Meeting House | |
| Lambert's, tavern | 41 | (Epis.) | 48 |
| Lattimore Ferry | 33 | Maning | 20 |
| Laughron | 67 | Marcus Hook | 52 |
| Lawrence, Cap. | 41 | Market house | 59 |
| Lawson's, tavern | 13 | Marrin's, tavern | 5 |
| Leary | 1 | Marshall | 4 |
| Lefurgy | 8 | Marsh's, grist mill | 41 |
| Legg | 30 | Marsh's, saw mill | 41 |
| Legget's, tavern | 1 | Martin | 83 |
| Lent | 10 | Martins or Cooks Run | 45 |
| Lent's, blacksmith shop | 10 | Marvin | 5 |
| Lent's, tavern | 10 | Marvin's, blacksmith shop | 5 |
| LeRoy | 20 | Mason | 10 |
| Lesten's, tavern | 9 | Massaponick River | 70 |
| Lilly, Cap. | 10 | Mattaponye River | 71, 72, 82, 83 |
| Lindsey | 85 | Mead (2) | 4 |
| Lippingwill | 49 | Mead, blacksmith shop | 4 |
| Lisle | 47* | Mead, Gen. | 3 |
| Little Crum Creek | 52 | Mead's, tavern | 4 |
| Little Elk Creek | 55 | Mead's, tavern | 11 |
| Little Gunpowder Creek | 58 | Meredecun Creek | 75 |

# ALPHABETICAL INDEX

| Name | Plate No. | Name | Plate No. |
|---|---|---|---|
| Merret's, tavern | 33 | Newcastle, Va. | 74 |
| Merits | 3 | New Kent Court House, Va. | 76 |
| Merrits | 10 | Newport, Del. | 53 |
| Mesier | 13 | Newtown, Conn. | 16 |
| Middlebrook, S. | 15 | Newtown, Md. | 57 |
| Middlesex, Conn. | 4 | New York City | 1 |
| Mill Creek | 51, 55, 56 | Niabscoe River | 67 |
| Mill Creek, grist mill | 51 | Nicholas | 4, 7 |
| Miller | 3, 13, 25, 45 | Nichols | 15 |
| Mills | 13 | Nichols, Esq. | 7 |
| Millstone River | 44 | Nichols', tavern | 7 |
| Mine Hole | 58 | Nile | 16 |
| Mingler | 22 | Nine Partners | 18 |
| Mitchel, Capt. | 18 | Noals Creek | 51 |
| Mizrol | 45* | Normans Kill | 26 |
| Moger's, tavern | 15 | North River | 9, 26, 32, 40 |
| Momaronek Bay | 3 | North East River | 55 |
| Montgomery, Gen. | 21 | North Run | 62 |
| Montier | 54 | Norwalk, Conn. | 5 |
| Moore | 44 | Nottingham Iron Works | 58 |
| Moorstown, N.J. | 49 | Noxon | 19 |
| Morehouse (2) | 6 | | |
| Morin | 1 | Oakley, grist mill | 11 |
| Morres | 1 | Occaquan Creek | 67 |
| Mount Holly, hill | 49 | Odell | 8 |
| Mount Hollytown, N.J. | 49 | Old Fairfield, Conn. | 7 |
| Mulliner | 33 | Old Furnace | 60 |
| Murder Creek | 25 | Old House | 6 |
| Murray | 1 | Old Meeting House (Presb.) | 23 |
| Musser | 62 | Osborne | 6 |
| Myers | 1 | Osborn's, tavern | 6 |
| Myer's, tavern | 2 | Ostrander's, tavern | 20, 31 |
| Myer's, tavern | 14 | Oswald, Col. | 52 |
| | | | |
| Naamans Creek | 52 | Palmar (2) | 3, 4 |
| Nash, gaol | 5 | Palmar, M., Esq. | 4 |
| Negro pens | 74 | Palmer's, Wid., tavern | 73 |
| Neil's, tavern | 1 | Palmetier | 20 |
| Neshammony Creek | 46 | Palnitz | 1 |
| New Rochell, N.Y. | 2 | Pamunky River | 74, 80 |
| Newark, N.J. | 40 | Parsons | 41 |
| Newborough, N.Y. | 33 | Parsons, blacksmith shop | 24 |

| Name | Plate No. | Name | Plate No. |
|---|---|---|---|
| Passaick River | 40 | Poughkeepsie, N.Y. | 14 |
| Patuxen River | 63 | Powder House | 1 |
| Paulus Hook, N.J. | 40 | Powels Run | 67 |
| Pawling | 21 | Powers (2) | 52 |
| Payton's, tavern | 68 | Presbyterian Church | |
| Pearsal's, tavern | 5 | (Near Capt. Booth) | 15 |
| Peck's, tavern | 4 | Princeton, N.J. | 44 |
| Peed, Wid. | 86 | Principio Creek | 56 |
| Peekskill, N.Y. | 11 | Purdle | 58 |
| Peet | 15 | Purdy (3) | 3 |
| Peet's, grist & fulling mill | 15 | Purdy | 33 |
| Pell, C. | 2 | | |
| Pell, D. | 2 | Quantocco Creek | 67 |
| Pell, P., Esq. | 2 | Quintard, blacksmith shop | 4 |
| Pelton | 4 | Quintard's, tavern | 5 |
| Peltz | 14 | | |
| Pemunky River | 73 | Rapahannock River | 69, 85 |
| see also Pamunky River | | Rapalje's, tavern | 12 |
| Pendleton's, tavern | 82 | Rappahanock River | 70 |
| Penfield's, tavern | 6 | see also Rapahannock River | |
| Pennsawkin Creek | 50 | Rariton River | 43 |
| Penny | 53 | Raway Meeting House (Epis.) | 41 |
| Person | 29 | Rawling's, grist mill | 63 |
| Philadelphia, Pa. | 47, 50, 51 | Rawling's, tavern | 61 |
| Philips', Capt., tavern | 58 | Rawson's, tavern | 76 |
| Philips's | 8 | Raymond | 4, 5 |
| Philips's, tavern | 44 | Raymond, Cap. | 5 |
| Pickett | 71 | Red Clay Creek | 53 |
| Pidgeon Swamp | 45* | Red Hook, N.J. | 22 |
| Pierson's, tavern | 40 | Red House | 59 |
| Piles | 52 | Red Lion, tavern | 46 |
| Pinkney | 2 | Reed | 4, 21 |
| Pintard | 2 | Reed's, tavern | 5 |
| Piscataway, N.J. | 43 | Relayer | 3 |
| Platt | 5 | Remarkable Spring | 13 |
| Platts | 4 | Renselaer, Esq. | 24 |
| Pollock, Wid. | 41 | Rhinelander | 2 |
| Port Royal, Va. | 85 | Rich | 8 |
| Post | 8 | Richards | 4 |
| Potowmack River | 65 | Ridley Creek | 2 |
| Potowmack Run | 69 | Ridley's Burnt House | 48 |
| Potter's, tavern | 42 | Ripley | 5 |

| Name | Plate No. | Name | Plate No. |
|---|---|---|---|
| Rising Sun, N.J. | 48 | Shabbacunk Creek | 45 |
| Robert | 8 | Shearman (2) | 7 |
| Robertson | 52 | Sheldon's, tavern | 18 |
| Robeson, mill | 53 | Shippetawkin Brook | 44 |
| Rocceau | 2 | Shute's, tavern | 13 |
| Rocky Brook | 46° | Simson's, blacksmith shop | 14 |
| Rocky Hill | 44 | Skelton | 74 |
| Rocky Hill Mills | 44 | Slabtown, N.J. | 48 |
| Rogers | 19, 56 | Slimets | 8 |
| Rogers', tavern | 11 | Slingland | 26 |
| Rogers Pond | 19 | Slover | 43 |
| Rollin | 61 | Smith | 21, 29, 45 |
| Roosevelt | 2 | Smith's, tavern | 33 |
| Rose | 2 | Sneed's, tavern | 84 |
| Roton River | 4 | Snowdens Ironworks | 64 |
| Roundout Kill | 31 | Somes's, tavern | 20 |
| Rowel | 16 | South River, Head of | 63 |
| Ruffins Ferry | 80 | Southard | 12 |
| Russel, Esq. | 55 | Squib | 52 |
| Rye, N.Y. | 3 | Squire & Mostin | 6 |
| Rynbeck Flats | 21 | Staatsborough | 21 |
| Rynbeck Mill | 22 | Stafford Court House, Va. | 68 |
|  |  | Stamford, Conn. | 4 |
| Sagatuck Bridge | 5 | Stars, tavern | 17 |
| Sagerches | 30 | Steenbergh | 21, 30 |
| St. James's Church (Epis.) | 51 | Stiths | 86 |
| Sampinck Brook | 46° | Stone Creek | 52 |
| Sampinck Creek | 45 | Stoney Brook | 44 |
| Sandersons Mill Creek | 85 | Stoney Brook Grist Mill | 44 |
| Sandiminian Church | 16 | Storm | 9 |
| Saw Pits | 3 | Storms | 8 |
| Schirmerhorn | 22 | Story | 46° |
| Scofield | 4 | Stoutenburgh | 14 |
| School | 15, 17, 33, 46°, 47°, 49 | Stoutenburgh, Widow | 14 |
| School House (W. of Stratford) | 7 | Stratford, Conn. | 15 |
| Schoonmaker | 13 | Strawthers | 85 |
| Schop | 21 | Striker | 45° |
| Schuyler, Gen. | 26 | Summe | 7 |
| Schuylkill River | 51 | Susquehannah River | 56 |
| Scott, Dr. | 61 | Sutton | 42 |
| Selby | 63 | Sutton's, tavern | 3 |
| Seward | 4 | Swaine | 51 |

| Name | Plate No. | Name | Plate No. |
|------|------|------|------|
| Swan Creek | 56 | Valkenburgh | 25 |
| Swartwout's, mill | 14 | Valkenburgh's, tavern | 28 |
| Swartwout's, tavern | 20 | Van Alen | 24 |
| Sydam | 43 | Van Bergen | 26 |
| | | Vanbergen, Col. | 28 |
| Tamage | 9 | Van Bunschoten, | |
| Tarrytown, N.Y. | 9 | blacksmith shop | 13 |
| Tater's, tavern | 22 | Van Bremer | 1 |
| Taunton Pond | 16 | Vancleve | 45 |
| Taylor's, grist mill | 80 | Vandegrift | 46 |
| Taylor's, tavern | 5 | Van D. Water, mill | 20 |
| Tenbrook | 31 | Van Hart | 46 |
| Terrel's, tavern | 41 | Van Leva | 43 |
| Thiel (2) | 3 | Van Ness | 23 |
| Thomas's, tavern | 22 | Van Ness, Maj. | 22 |
| Thornton | 70 | Vanorden | 29 |
| Thornton, Wid. | 71 | Van Tassel | 9, 10 |
| The 3 Tuns, tavern | 52 | Van Vlict | 31 |
| Tiebout | 1 | Van Weart | 9 |
| Tilthorn | 33 | Vanweghtens | 29 |
| Titus | 4 | Van Wies | 27 |
| Titus Bridge | 4 | Van Wyck's, tavern (2) | 12 |
| Todd's, tavern | 70 | Van Zandt | 1 |
| Todd's Bridge | 82 | Vermilyea | 10 |
| Tombs's, tavern | 85 | Vincent | 2 |
| Tomkins | 32 | | |
| Totopotomoy Creek | 74 | Waldron | 43 |
| Towers | 51 | Waldron's, tavern | 1 |
| Toy | 50 | Walker | 15 |
| Travers's, tavern | 11 | Wappings Creek | 20 |
| Trenton, N.J. | 45 | Wappins Kill | 13 |
| Trenton Ferry | 45 | Ward's, tavern | 9 |
| Trimper's, tavern | 21 | Ward's, tavern | 46* |
| Tucker | 41 | Waring | 4 |
| Tully | 45 | Warren, blacksmith shop | 11 |
| Turney (2) | 15 | Washington's, Gen. | 66 |
| Tussey | 53 | Watkins | 1 |
| Tuttle | 10 | Wattle | 11 |
| | | Webb's, tavern | 4 |
| Uffoot | 15 | Weeks, Esq. | 12 |
| | | Weeks's, tavern | 12 |
| Valentine | 76 | Wells | 30 |

# ALPHABETICAL INDEX

| Name | Plate No. | Name | Plate No. |
|---|---|---|---|
| Wentworth | 5 | Williamson | 43 |
| West Camp | 29, 30 | Wilmington, Del. | 53 |
| Wetherell | 45* | Wilmington Academy | 53 |
| Wetherington's, grist mill | 62 | Winters Run | 57 |
| Wheat Sheaf, tavern | 41, 47 | Woodbridge | 42 |
| White Clay Creek | 53 | Wright | 5 |
| White house | 44 | Wykoff | 43 |
| Whiting | 4 | | |
| Whitlock at | | Yarnton | 32 |
| Hudibras, tavern | 43 | Yates | 23 |
| Whitmore | 3, 4 | York, Va. | 79 |
| Whitney's, tavern | 32 | York River | 79 |
| Williams | 2 | Young's, tavern | 4 |
| Williamsburgh, Va. | 78 | Young's, tavern | 33 |

# Classified Index

## BLACKSMITH SHOPS

| Name or Location | Plate No. | Name or Location | Plate No. |
|---|---|---|---|
| *near* Benedict | 5 | Norwalk, Conn. | 5 |
| Coopers | 12 | *near* Noxon | 19 |
| Danbury | 17 | Old Fairfield, Conn. | 7 |
| Dorland | 19 | *north of* Palmar | 3 |
| Fish Kill, N.Y. | 12 | Parsons | 24 |
| Flandreau | 3 | Quintard | 4 |
| Gidney | 3 | *west of* Rye, N.Y. | 3 |
| Lent | 10 | Simsons | 14 |
| *near* Mason | 10 | Van Bunschoten | 13 |
| Mead | 4 | *near* Walker | 15 |
| New Rochell, N.Y. | 2 | Warren | 11 |
| Newtown, Conn. | 16 | | |

## CHURCHES

### Episcopal

| Name or Location | Plate No. | Name or Location | Plate No. |
|---|---|---|---|
| Alexandria, Va. | 65 | Moorstown, N.J. | 49 |
| Brick Church | 81 | Newtown, Conn. | 16 |
| Bristol, N.J. | 46 | Norwalk, Conn. | 5 |
| Danbury, Conn. | 17 | *near* Philips's | 8 |
| Elizabethtown, N.J. | 41 | Piscataway, N.J. | 43 |
| Fish Kill, N.Y. | 12 | Raway Meeting House | 41 |
| Frankford, N.J. | 47 | St. James | 51 |
| Hickory Nut Church | 77 | Stamford, Conn. | 4 |
| Horses Neck, Conn. | 4 | Stratford, Conn. | 15 |
| Mansfield Meeting House | 48 | | |

### Presbyterian

| Name or Location | Plate No. | Name or Location | Plate No. |
|---|---|---|---|
| *near* Cap. Booth | 15 | Horses Neck, Conn. | 4 |
| Cranberry, N.J. | 46* | Kenderhook, N.Y. | 24 |
| Danbury, Conn. | 17 | Kingston, N.J. | 44 |
| Dutch Church, Presb. | 43 | Kooksachke, N.Y. | 28 |
| Fairfield, Conn. | 6 | Maidenhead, N.J. | 44 |
| Fish Kill, N.Y. | 12 | Middlesex, Conn. | 4 |

## CHURCHES (continued)

| Name or Location | Plate No. | Name or Location | Plate No. |
|---|---|---|---|
| New Rochell, N.Y. | 2 | Poughkeepsie, N.Y. | 14 |
| Newark, N.J. | 40 | Princeton, N.J. | 44 |
| Norwalk, Conn. | 5 | Stamford, Conn. | 4 |
| Old Fairfield, Conn. | 7 | Stratford, Conn. | 15 |
| Old Meeting House | 23 | | |

### Other

| Name or Location | Plate No. | Name or Location | Plate No. |
|---|---|---|---|
| Albany, Dutch Church | 26 | Crosswicks, N.J. Quaker | |
| Baptist Meeting House | 41 | Meeting House | 47* |
| Claverack Meeting House | 23 | Sandiminian Church | 16 |

## DOCTORS

| Name | Plate No. | Name | Plate No. |
|---|---|---|---|
| Dr. Bard | 21 | Dr. Kierstead | 30 |
| Dr. Bland | 41 | Dr. Scott | 61 |
| Dr. Cooper | 21 | | |

## INDUSTRIES

| Name | Plate No. | Name | Plate No. |
|---|---|---|---|
| Iron Works | | Snowdens | 64 |
| Kingsbury | 59 | Pottery plant | 3 |
| Nottingham | 58 | Powder House | 1 |
| Old Furnace | 60 | | |

## MILLS

| Name | Plate No. | Name | Plate No. |
|---|---|---|---|
| Boring | | Aylett's | 82 |
| near Fredericksburg, Va. | 69 | Booth | 55 |
| Flax | | Booth's, Capt. | 15 |
| Stamford, Conn. | 4 | Boutten | 4 |
| Fulling | | Bownes | 3 |
| near Hunts | 8 | Bushtown, Md. | 57 |
| Knaps | 6 | Cortlandt | 8 |
| Peets | 15 | Cranberry, N.J. | 46* |
| Stamford, Conn. | 4 | Dennis's | 19 |
| Grist | | Drake's, Col. | 9 |
| Adams's | 65 | Frankford, N.J. | 47 |
| Allentown, Pa. | 47* | Freligh | 21 |

## MILLS (continued)

| Name or Location | Plate No. | Name or Location | Plate No. |
|---|---|---|---|
| Gray's | 63 | Rawling's | 63 |
| Hightstown, N.J. | 46* | Robeson's | 53 |
| Hooe's | 86 | Rynbeck, N.Y. | 22 |
| Hunt's | 3 | Sampinck Creek | 45 |
| Huntingdon | 2 | Stoney brook | 44 |
| Inglis | 49 | Swartwout's | 14 |
| Knap's | 6 | Taylor's | 80 |
| McElwaine's | 52 | Van D. Water | 20 |
| Marsh's | 41 | Wetherington's | 62 |
| Mill Creek | 51 | Saw | |
| near New York State line | 17 | Marsh's | 41 |
| Norwalk, Conn. | 5 | Saw Pits | 3 |
| Oakley's | 11 | Tub | |
| Peet's | 15 | Johnson's | 75 |
| Quantocco Creek | 67 | | |

## SCHOOLS and COLLEGES

| Name or Location | Plate No. | Name or Location | Plate No. |
|---|---|---|---|
| near Crosswicks, N.J. | 47* | Stratford, Conn. | 15 |
| Danbury, Conn. | 17 | west of Stratford | 7 |
| near Hightstown, N.J. | 46* | William and Mary College, | |
| near Mount Hollytown, N.J. | 49 | Williamsburgh, Va. | 78 |
| near Newborough, N.Y. | 33 | Wilmington Academy | 53 |
| Princeton (College), N.J. | 44 | | |

## STORES and WAREHOUSES

| Name or Location | Plate No. | Name or Location | Plate No. |
|---|---|---|---|
| Aylett's Warehouse | 82 | Ponsall's Store | 5 |
| Clifts Store | 5 | | |

## TAVERNS

| Name or Location | Plate No. | Name or Location | Plate No. |
|---|---|---|---|
| Adamson's | 1 | Archer's | 8 |
| Alleckson at | | Aukard's | 61 |
| Crooked Billet | 46* | Baker's | 41 |
| The Anchor | 52 | Baldwin's | 63 |

## TAVERNS (continued)

| Name or Location | Plate No. | Name or Location | Plate No. |
|---|---|---|---|
| Baldwin's, Col. | 16 | Drake's | 9 |
| Beech's | 15 | Duncastle or | |
| The Bell | 51 | Bird's Ordinary | 77 |
| Bennet's | 15 | Dusenbury's | 8 |
| Bett's | 5 | Dusenbury's | 11 |
| Bird's | 55 | Erwin's | 51 |
| Bird's Ordinary | | Fish Kill, N.Y. (3) | 12 |
| see Duncastle Ordinary | | Fore's | 44 |
| Birdsall's | 10 | Fosburg's | 24 |
| Blackman | 16 | Fraer's | 13 |
| Blue Ball | 52 | Frank's | 80 |
| Blue Bull | 54 | Frenck's | 15 |
| Blue Horse | 42 | Gardner's Ordinary | 83 |
| Borrum's | 14 | Gen. Washington, The | 50 |
| Boscawen's, Adm. | 53 | Grierson's | 1 |
| Bowling Green Ordinary | 71 | Halfway-House Ordinary | 79 |
| Boyan's | 60 | Haley | 15 |
| Brook's | 15 | Halsey's | 2 |
| Brownell's | 18 | Haviland's | 3 |
| Burk's | 58 | Head Lynch | 72 |
| Burnt Brick Ordinary | 77 | Hendrick's & Pool's | 14 |
| Burnt Ordinary | 82 | Higby's | 50 |
| Burrel's | 5 | Hinman's | 15 |
| Chandler's, Gen. | 16 | Hollingworth's | 55 |
| Clark's, Cap. | 17 | Holmes's | 47 |
| Clawson's | 43 | Hopkin's | 18 |
| Cook's | 18 | Horton's | 3 |
| Cooper's | 12 | Howel's | 56 |
| Couenhoven's | 45 | Hugin's | 18 |
| Covenhoven's | 9 | Hunt's | 8 |
| Craig's | 41 | Hyatt's | 2 |
| Crawford's | 2 | Kelsey's | 14 |
| Danbury, Conn. (2) | 17 | Kenner's Red House | 72 |
| Day's | 1 | Knap's | 4 |
| Dean's | 1 | Konyn's | 28 |
| Delezeune's | 9 | Lambert's | 41 |
| Delong's | 19 | Lamb's | 19 |
| Demot's | 33 | Lawson's | 13 |
| Dennis's | 19 | Legget's | 1 |
| Devoe's | 32 | Lent's | 10 |

## TAVERNS (*continued*)

| Name or Location | Plate No. | Name or Location | Plate No. |
|---|---|---|---|
| Lesten's | 9 | Red Lion | 46 |
| McCalley's | 49 | Reed's | 5 |
| McCracken's | 44 | Roger's | 11 |
| McCurdy's | 56 | Sheldon's | 18 |
| Marrin's | 5 | Shute's | 13 |
| Mead's | 4 | Smith's | 33 |
| Mead's | 11 | Sneed's | 84 |
| Merret's | 33 | Somes's | 20 |
| Moger's | 15 | Stamford, Conn. | 4 |
| Myer's | 2 | Stars | 17 |
| Myer's | 14 | Stratford, Conn. (2) | 15 |
| Neil's | 1 | Sutton's | 3 |
| Newark, N.J. | 40 | Swartwout's | 20 |
| Newtown, Conn. | 16 | Tater's | 22 |
| Nichol's | 7 | Taylor's | 5 |
| Norman's | 26 | Terrel's | 41 |
| Old Fairfield, Conn. | 7 | Thomas's | 22 |
| Osborn's | 6 | The 3 Tuns | 52 |
| Ostrander's | 20 | Todd's | 70 |
| Ostrander's | 31 | Tombs's | 85 |
| Palmer's, Wid. | 73 | Travers's | 11 |
| Payton's | 68 | Trimper's | 21 |
| Peck's | 4 | Valkenburgh's | 28 |
| Pendleton's | 82 | Van Wyck's (2) | 12 |
| Penfield's | 6 | Waldron's | 1 |
| Philips's | 44 | Ward's | 9 |
| Philips's, Capt. | 58 | Ward's | 46* |
| Pierson's | 40 | Webb's | 4 |
| Potter's | 42 | Weeks's | 12 |
| Poughkeepsie, N.Y. (3) | 14 | Wheat Sheaf | 41, 47 |
| Quintard's | 5 | Whitlock at Hudibras | 43 |
| Rapalje's | 12 | Whitney's | 32 |
| Rawling's | 61 | Young's | 4 |
| Rawson's | 76 | Young's | 33 |

# Index to Part One

Adams, John, 100

Adgate, Mr. (New York State Assemblyman), 27

American Museum, 89

American Philosophical Society, 7, 10, 11, 12

Banks (of the Commissary Dept., Continental Army), 18

Biddle, Owen, 11

Brown, Mr. (New York State Assemblyman), 50

Buel, John, 83

Burgoyne, Gen. John, 63

Butler, Col. William, 48, 49, 63

Carey, Mathew, 102

Church, Elihu D., 59

Clinton, Gov. DeWitt, 31, 94

Clinton, Gen. George, 70

Clinton, Gen. James, 63

Clowes, Mr. (New York State Assemblyman), 50

Clymer, George, 62

Colden, Cadwallader D., 94

Collect Pond, 13

Colles, Dr. Christopher John, 92

Colles, Eliza, 60, 81

Colles, John, 16, 18, 81

Colles, Richard, 81

Colles, William, 4, 6

Connecticut River Surveys, 82

Continental Army, 59, 61, 66, 67; Artillery Department, 20, 24, 41, 42, 65, 72; Geographers Department, 24, 60, 63

Continental Congress, 62, 68, 69, 71

Cornwallis, Gen. Charles, 67

Davidson, Eliza N. Pintard, 90

DeWitt, Richard Varick, 70

DeWitt, Simeon, 19, 24, 53, 54, 55, 63, 65, 66, 67, 68, 69, 70, 71, 72

Dukart, Mr. (Engineer, Limerick, Ireland), 4

Electric machines, 36

Erie Canal, 31

Erskine, Robert, 19, 24, 54, 55, 62, 63, 64, 65, 70, 76

Erskine-DeWitt maps, 55, 57, 60, 64, 65, 70, 73, 75, 76, 104

Federal Hall, 100

Fig blue manufactory, 26, 36

Fitch, John, 12

Fourth Pennsylvania Regiment, 48, 63

Francis, Dr. John W., 19, 84, 90, 92, 94, 95

Frothingham, James, 92

Geographers Department, see Continental Army, Geographers Department

Geographers of the United States, see Continental Army, Geographers Department

Geographical Ledger and Systematized Atlas, 79, 82, 83

Geography, lectures on, 7

Gerry, Elbridge, 62

Gray, Capt. William, 63

Great Lakes, 29, 31

Griscomb, John, 89

Gunnery, lectures on, 17, 37

Halsey's Tavern, 37

Hamilton, Col. Alexander, 21, 24, 42

Harper, Mr. (New York State Assemblyman), 27
Havens, Mr. (New York State Assemblyman), 50
Heath, James, 46
Hosack, Dr. David, 94
Hutchins, Thomas, 21

Jarvis, John Wesley, 92
Jefferson, Thomas, 35, 69, 77

Keough, Anne, 4
King, Charles, 94
Kingston, New York, burning of, 18, 20
Knox, Gen. Henry, 20, 21, 24, 42, 70, 71, 72

Lafayette, Marquis de, 42
Lamb, Anthony, 16
Lamb, Gen. John, 16, 17, 18, 20, 21, 24, 37, 42, 48, 70, 72, 84
Limerick, Ireland, Colles' plan of, 6
Livingston, Philip, 62
Lodge, Lt. Benjamin, 63
Loudon, Samuel, 29

Mercereau's "Flying Machine," 97
Metropolitan Museum of Art, 92
Microscope, solar, see Solar microscope
Military geographers, see Continental Army, Geographers Department
Mohawk River navigation improvement proposal, 26, 27, 29, 31, 32, 36, 49
Morse, Samuel, 89

Natural philosophy, lectures on, 10, 12
New York Academy of Fine Arts, 89
New York City, Common Council, 13, 19, 25, 26, 36, 88

New York City, map by Cornelius Tiebout, 46
New York City water supply project, 13, 16, 18, 19, 25, 83
New-York Historical Society, 65, 70, 72, 89, 92, 104
New York Institution, 89, 90
New York Society Library, 89
New York State Legislature, 27, 29, 50, 59, 60

Ogilby, John, 73
Ohio River navigation improvement proposal, 21, 25, 26
Osgood, Samuel, 50, 51, 52, 69
Ossory, Bishop of, 4; see also Pococke, Dr. Richard
Oswald, Col. Eleazer, 18

Paine, Mr. (New York State Assemblyman), 27
Perambulator, 42, 43, 45, 50, 51, 52, 53, 59, 100
Peutinger Table, 75
Philosophical Society of New York, 89
Pickering, Col. Timothy, 66
Pintard, John, 81, 84, 90, 92
Pococke, Dr. Richard, 4, 19
Prescott, Benjamin, 83
Proud, Robert, 11

Quebec, Battle of, 17

Remsen, Henry, 21, 27
Rittenhouse, David, 11

St. Paul's Episcopal Church, churchyard, 90, 94
Schuyler, Gen. Philip, 17, 65
Scudder, John, 89
Semaphoric telegraph, see Telegraph, semaphoric
Solar microscope, 37, 40, 85

Sons of Liberty, 16, 41, 84
South Hadley Falls Canal, 82, 83
Steam engine, 10, 11, 12, 13
Steuben, Baron von, 64
Sullivan, Gen. John, 20, 49, 65
Sullivan's Expedition, 20, 49, 63

Teabout, Cornelius, 48, 49; *see also* Tiebout, Cornelius
Telegraph, semaphoric, 85, 87, 88, 89
Thompson, Mr. (New York State Assemblyman), 27
Ticonderoga, Battle of, 17
Tiebout, Cornelius, 45, 46, 48, 49, 60
Tiebout, Elizabeth Lamb, 48
Tiebout, Tunis, 48
Timber canal proposal, 32, 35, 84
Trumbull, Jonathan, 68
Turners Falls Canal, 82

United States: Congress, 42, 50, 59, 60; Postmaster General, 50, 51, 52, 59; Post Office Department, 50, 51; Secretary of War, 68; War Department, 70, 71
United States Census, 1790, 100
United States Military and Philosophical Society, 89

Vaughn, Gen. John, 18

War of 1812, 88
Washington, Gen. George, 19, 21, 24, 25, 37, 42, 53, 54, 55, 60, 61, 62, 64, 66, 67, 68, 69, 70, 71, 77, 84, 100
Wells, Richard, 11
Williamson, Hugh, 69
Wire-works, 15
Wood Creek, 27

Yorktown, Battle of, 17, 42, 67

# THE JOHN HARVARD LIBRARY

*The intent of*
*Waldron Phoenix Belknap, Jr.,*
*as expressed in an early will, was for*
*Harvard College to use the income from a*
*permanent trust fund he set up, for "editing and*
*publishing rare, inaccessible, or hitherto unpublished*
*source material of interest in connection with the*
*history, literature, art (including minor and useful*
*art), commerce, customs, and manners or way of*
*life of the Colonial and Federal Periods of the United*
*States . . . In all cases the emphasis shall be on the*
*presentation of the basic material." A later testament*
*broadened this statement, but Mr. Belknap's inter-*
*ests remained constant until his death.*

*In linking the name of the first benefactor of*
*Harvard College with the purpose of this later,*
*generous-minded believer in American culture the*
*John Harvard Library seeks to emphasize the impor-*
*tance of Mr. Belknap's purpose. The John Harvard*
*Library of the Belknap Press of Harvard University*
*Press exists to make books and documents*
*about the American past more readily*
*available to scholars and the*
*general reader.*